THE WINNING MIND

THE WINNING MIND

A Guide to Achieving Success and Overcoming Failure

Steve Backley
with Ian Stafford

AURUM PRESS

First published 1996
by Aurum Press Ltd, 25 Bedford
Avenue, London WC1B 3AT

A catalogue record for this book is available from the British Library.

ISBN 1 85410 404 7

2 4 6 8 10 9 7 5 3 1
1997   1999   2000   1998   1996

Typeset by Computerset, Hamondsworth
Printed in Great Britain by Hartnolls Ltd, Bodmin

CONTENTS

ACKNOWLEDGEMENTS ....

Although I am an individual sportsman who has gained prominence in a sport designed primarily for individuals, there have been many, many people over the years who have contributed to the success I have achieved in world athletics.

If I was to name everybody who has played a part in my success then the list might well be longer than the book you are about to read. But I would like to say a very big 'thank you' to all the trainers, physiotherapists, psychologists, team-mates, training partners, advisors, doctors, masseurs and friends for all their hard and excellent work on my behalf.

I would like to add a special word of thanks to my father, John, for his relentless support, and to my coach, John Trower, who has devoted so much time and effort to my cause.

Steve Backley, 6 January 1996.

INTRODUCTION

....

You may not have really thought about this before, but, like it or not, psychology plays a critical part in everybody's day-to-day life. It is in the use of your mind – either consciously or subconsciously – that you can ultimately decide whether you eventually achieve your goals in sport, and indeed in life. Your mind has the power to make you a winner.

Psychology has played an increasingly large role in my own event – throwing the javelin. It has the same part to play whether you are, potentially, a top sportsperson, or just a recreational player who enjoys a weekly game of squash, a Sunday morning league football match, or a round of golf.

But, of course, psychology can play a crucial role in areas far beyond sport. I have benefited from using what is known as sports psychology because sport happens to be my profession, but I have also consciously manipulated my mind in order to achieve greater levels of performance in business, in the media and in everyday life.

If you are facing a job interview, for example, your mind needs to be in the best possible shape. If you are on the verge of cracking an important business deal for either yourself or your company, it is your state of mind that can swing the final outcome. I would, therefore, not want anyone to jump to the conclusion that this book is relevant only to people who participate in sport at the highest level, or, indeed, that the principles of sports psychology are relevant exclusively to sport.

By outlining the basic theories and principles behind good, sound sports psychology, and by introducing you to some of the techniques that can help you make better use of your mind, you should be able to take from this book advice that you can apply not only in a sporting situation but also in everyday situations where mental application is required.

So, before you think – This is all very well, but Backley competes in the Olympics, that's a different planet to the one I live on – consider this: we all have a talent, and we all have a mind, but not many of us know how to discover our talent, or really fulfil our potential.

I am only too well aware that the whole subject of 'psychology' has been seen by many to be a bit of a turn-off. It conjures up images of white-coated, wild-haired boffins staring into a model of a brain, or unstable characters, such as Robbie Coltrane's 'Fitz' in the hit television drama series Cracker.

Many of you who have studied psychology, as I did as part of my Sports Science degree course back in the late 1980s at Loughborough University, may not even have considered it to be one of the mainstream subjects. 'Proper' degree courses were subjects such as Law and Medicine, which paved the way into one of the more accepted 'professions'.

Well, this whole perception of psychology has now changed. It has always been with us, of course, but now people, particularly in sport, have woken up to the fact that psychology, if understood, developed and utilized in the correct fashion, can become a major contributing factor towards success. Rather like nutrition, diet and sports injury and rehabilitation clinics, psychology is now fully accepted and used in sport.

Today, it is better understood as a process by which we try to attain our goals, and its basic principles apply in every field and walk of life. The next step is to accept it *consciously* in life.

Without wishing to criticize other psychology authors, I have found many books on the subject to be too academic, their pages filled with too much jargon and theory. As a result, they have been of only moderate use to the general public. Where I hope this book is different is that I am going not only to provide you with the theories, but, also, by referring to my own ups and downs in the world of sport, I am going to help you translate them into practice.

After all, we have all succeeded in the past when we 'felt in the right mood' or just 'couldn't put a foot wrong', just as we have failed because 'we didn't feel like it', or 'knew it wasn't going to be our day'. If we are totally honest with ourselves, we know that the critical factor in such instances was not our physical well-being, nor was it just down to good or bad luck – it was to do with our *mental* state.

This is common in sport. When people take up a sport they generally work hard on physical aspects that will help improve their performance. Consequently, many sports are littered with people who are physically very fit but who are incapable of implementing the crucial mental skills – and this has an effect not only on the state of their mind, but also on their ability to learn a technique.

Of course, I am not suggesting that a knowledge of how to use psychology is all you need to become an instant winner in whatever you do. If this was the case, and I had all the answers, then I would be winning every single competition I entered. We all know that is impossible. There are a host of reasons why I can finish in second place, or worse, but because of my experiences, I am now less likely to put any failure down to my mental state. And even if I do, then at least I will be sure to understand why it happened, and I'll be able to do something about it in order to prevent it from happening again.

So, the message of this book is that your state of mind is not something you simply have to accept. You can stop your mind working against you, and you can encourage it to work for you. It all boils down to how well you understand – and how well you can manipulate – your own psychology. The fact is that you and your mind are inseparable, so you may as well learn how to become compatible.

My own career has, to date, provided a catalogue of examples of where my mind has worked either for or against my efforts to attain my goals. I therefore believe, in this introductory chapter, that it is relevant to assess my own sporting curriculum vitae to underline just how much your mental state can affect your final performance.

From an early age the best way I found to express myself was through sport. I have always possessed a great desire to win and, as far back as I can remember, the attraction of sport was the thrill of competition, rather than the practicalities of running, jumping, kicking, or whatever else I might have been up to.

I have tried most sports, and just about every discipline in athletics, but because I have always been big I was best suited to the throwing events. I remember harassing a school teacher into dropping someone from the school under-15s athletics team in favour of me in the shot putt. I went on to record three no-throws, which left me ashamed and embarrassed. But it also made me determined to bounce back and, in the next competition, I beat the school's champion.

My next step was to enter the local schools' District Championships. A friend of mine was, on paper, better than me. He could throw 15 metres, while I could only manage 13.5 metres, but when we faced each other in competition I somehow managed to come up with a throw of 15.20 metres in the first round. I went on to win with that throw.

Already, even though I was barely a teenager, I had learned a useful psychological tactic, which I have tried to employ in competition ever since. Get a good throw in as quickly as possible. If you are a long jumper, get your best leap in first. This immediately puts extra pressure on the opposition. More often than not this works, whether at the Olympics or at school level. It not only sets a precedent for yourself, but also changes the way you are viewed by your opposition and thus gives you an immediate competitive advantage.

It soon became obvious that the javelin was my best event. I went on to win the Kent Championships and, in just my second year of throwing, I finished up second in the English Schools Championships. I went one better the following year, which set me up for the 1987 European Junior Championships in Birmingham.

I remember the day of competition at the European Championships vividly. The weather was dreadful. It was rainy and windy, conditions that immediately put most sports people off, but not me. For some reason, I actually prefer it when the conditions are apparently against you. I think this is because I know the havoc the conditions are playing on the opposition's mind. They decide, even before they start the event, that they cannot possibly do well. I find myself making exactly the same mistake in something like golf, where foul weather often results in a high-scoring round.

I can remember my father instilling this idea into my head from an early age. We went out running in the local woods during a heavy winter shower. My head was down at the prospect of having to train in a storm, until my father pointed out that those are the training sessions in which a champion is made, because it is certain that others will not bother. My father played an important role in the development of my outlook on sport. He helped create a mind that had the desire to win.

I proceeded to win the European Juniors, which, you would think, should have put me in good stead for the World Junior Championships in Sudbury, Canada, the following year. Instead, I allowed some external problems to affect me, first physically and then, more importantly, mentally. As a result, I experienced my first failure and disappointment in international sport.

I entered the competition as the clear favourite, especially after I had already broken the world junior record earlier that summer. But when the actual competition began, my head was suddenly filled with negative thoughts, which were to prove costly.

My main rival was a Russian called Vladimir Ovchinikov, whose best ever throw was a good three metres behind mine. Yet, in being the Gold Medal favourite, I found myself constantly looking over my shoulder. This is the extra pressure that a favourite is under, because he or she is expected to win, and anything else is seen as a failure. In short, I reacted very differently to how I had in any other competition that I had experienced in the past. I suddenly became aware of the searing heat, and felt a tremendous tiredness. Then, the wind started to gust from the left, and, when it blew over a measuring device, it delayed the event for 40 minutes; I sat down and became consumed with negative thoughts. Suddenly, I had convinced myself that everything was going wrong, and that everything was working against me. The end result? I finished second to Ovchinikov, which, to me, was a failure. Worse still, it was a failure that I can put down purely to mental factors.

This experience has stayed with me ever since, even though I was to suffer from more setbacks in my later career. If you fail mentally, then that says something about you as a person. I always take mental failure as a personal insult because, harsh as it sounds, I have let myself down. To fail mentally is far worse than losing for physical reasons.

The summer did not get any better. Although I was not really expected to qualify for the 1988 Seoul Olympics, I still harboured aspirations to make the British team, even if I was only 18. In the event, I finished fourth in the AAA's Championships, the official Olympic trials, and just missed out on a place.

It was as a result of this depressing summer that I first realized that there might have been something missing in my performance that I really needed to look into. I had a place waiting for me at Loughborough University to read Sports Science, which included sports psychology. It was here that I first became aware of the subject.

There were many times when I found the subject heavy going. I asked myself why I was having to analyse so much the very thing I simply wanted to get out and experience. For all the theories, putting psychology into practice is a very personal business because every personality differs, and everyone has different experiences. Still, this was the first time that I had been introduced to the theory of arousal, and to the relaxation and visualization technique that I will examine later in this book.

The winter of 1988 proved to be extremely productive for me. I found myself in an environment at Loughborough, surrounded by other, like-minded athletes, which was very conducive to training and preparation for the coming season, my first in senior athletics.

As a result, the 1989 season proved to be enormously successful. I won the World Cup, the Grand Prix javelin competition, was ranked third overall in the world of athletics, and grabbed British and Commonwealth records. It was very much a case of mixing with the big boys after my disappointing year 12 months earlier.

I suppose the reasons for this sudden improvement are straightforward. At 19, I had filled out and stopped growing. I suddenly possessed far greater strength, and became more explosive and powerful, which are the key elements to successful javelin throwing.

Psychology did not, however, at least not consciously, play a part. I suppose that when you are winning at such a young and inexperienced age, you do not really question anything. I did not really understand or appreciate the pressures, and had little respect for losing. Although I had found the theories of sports psychology interesting at university, I came out of the classroom no different as a performer. Looking back, it was my first year as a senior, and I was not expected to win anything. In a sense, then, I turned from the top-rated junior who had everything to lose, to the fresh-faced senior who had everything to gain.

I went off to the Commonwealth games in Auckland in January 1990 as the world's number-one ranked javelin thrower, and promptly took the Gold Medal, beating my friend and compatriot, Mick Hill, into second place. It was the start of an incredible year.

In July 1990, I threw my first world record, recording a throw of 89.58 metres in Stockholm. A week later, the man who has since become my biggest rival, the Czech Republic's Jan Zelezny, threw 8 centimetres further. I then came back to recapture my world record in August at Crystal Palace, before going on to win a Gold Medal at the European Championships in Split. When I was voted the world's number one athlete for 1990, beating a whole host of famous names from around the world, everybody in the sport, from fellow athletes to coaches, administration to the media, all predicted that the world would be lying at my feet.

It was difficult not to agree with them. After all, I was winning everything. It had become a pleasant habit, and the memory of finishing second in the 1988 World Junior Championships and, more importantly, the lessons I should have learned from the experience, were swept under the carpet. I would not say I was arrogant, but I was looking forward to cleaning up at the World Championships and the Olympic Games.

In stark contrast, 1991 turned out to be an unmitigated disaster, in which my mind decided to play damaging tricks on me. There was nothing to hint at the misery that lay ahead. I had trained hard during the winter, suffered no injuries, and really felt that I was still on a winning roll. Then I heard that a Finnish thrower called Seppo Raty had broken my world record.

To say that I was shocked is an understatement. The news transformed me from a confident, almost blasé young man, into a determined athlete, hellbent on reclaiming what I saw as right-fully mine. In my first competition that summer, at a low-key meeting in Loughborough, I threw 88 metres, which was an impressive start to my campaign. At the second meeting, also at Loughborough, during the warm-up I threw what was, at that time, probably the second-longest throw ever, and I decided that I was definitely on for the world record. There was never any doubt in my mind about this. Halfway through the run-up for my first throw, I suddenly tore my adductor muscle and was forced to withdraw.

This was my first real experience of injury and, looking back now, it also signalled the rapid downward spiral of my mental state. I had the whole summer to look ahead to, and many major international meetings to compete in, and there I was, in front of three men and a dog at a comparatively meaningless meeting, going for absolute broke.

This was my first lesson in how physical problems can then become mental ones, and vice versa. Inhibition is very damaging for a sportsperson, and the mental damage an injury can cause is sometimes far greater than any physical damage.

My next mistake was my determination to bounce back. Instead of being patient, ensuring that I had recovered fully from injury, I entered a competition four weeks later, almost fit. It proved to be a totally new and damaging experience. Preparations for the competition had been dominated by the injury. I was so full of negative thoughts that when it came to my turn to throw, I held back, frightened that I might repeat my injury by trying 100 per cent. This attitude remained with me throughout the summer, worsening as I began to experience losing in various Grand Prix competitions.

With the glorious benefit of hindsight, and an understanding that I now possess, I see that mine was a physical problem that became a mental problem. My mind might well have been fine had I not injured myself, but having suffered a physical setback, I then created a much bigger problem for myself. In other words, I panicked.

The World Championships in Tokyo signified the biggest failure in my career. I had prepared badly, competing too much and pushing my injury too hard. Concerned about damaging myself during the qualifying rounds of the javelin, I purposefully held back, thinking that I would be more than good enough to qualify for the final, when it really mattered. Instead, my first throw fell short of the required distance needed to qualify, and I immediately panicked again. From that point on, I did not stand a chance and, two throws later, I was out of the World Championships, having not even made it to the final. In the space of a year, I had fallen from the world's best to an also-ran.

I knew that I had a physical problem, but, deep down, I also knew that it was not so bad that I could not even qualify for the final. I remember – having already taken my frustration out in the baseball nets close to the stadium – that I returned to the athletes' village and threw my shoes out of the window in disgust.

I was desperate to make amends and, two weeks later in Sheffield, kept the promise I had made to myself. Not only did I win the competition, beating all three World Championship medallists in the process, but I smashed the Commonwealth record with a throw of 91.36 metres, a distance that would have won me the Gold Medal a fortnight before.

People were slapping me on the back and congratulating me for my performance, but I walked out of the stadium with my head down. I had just proved that my problems in Tokyo were not physical. I was ashamed of myself. I had let myself down badly, and I had no way of turning back the clock.

During the next winter I became very motivated and positive.

I entered a competition in New Zealand and broke the world record again, a direct result of my much-improved frame of mind. Ironically, Jan Zelezny took it away from me again in the summer. He too had bombed out of the 1991 World Championships qualifying round, but he had managed to get his act together the following year.

Despite this, my attitude seemed to be okay when I arrived at the 1992 Barcelona Olympics. I did not realize it at the time, but my preparation had once again been too severe, and I was physically run down. During the qualifying round, I injured myself slightly. It was nothing serious, but it meant that I entered the Olympic final with a problem.

It is hard for me to define how big a part my mind played in the final result. I remained – at least consciously – positive, until I tore my adductor again during my fourth-round throw, which, effectively, ended my challenge. I don't like to admit it, but I possibly had doubts because I knew I was not 100 per cent fit. Winning a Bronze Medal at the Olympics is not exactly a disaster, but having started the year by breaking the world record, I was aiming for gold.

The season ended in pain. My shoulder was hurting, I had nicked my elbow badly, and I had another adductor problem. As soon as I stopped throwing, my shoulder seized up, rather like an engine running out of oil. This necessitated an operation at the end of 1992, which left me thinking, throughout most of 1993, that I was finished as an athlete. This proved to be my darkest period, a time when a positive frame of mind would really have helped me to come through.

Instead, I was experiencing the most negative phase of my life. Mentally, I was torn apart, because I thought I was history. I was in so much pain that I used to wake up in the middle of the night and walk around to try to ease it. I just could not seem to lift my arm. Carrying out mundane actions, such as brushing my teeth, or trying to throw money into the automatic trough at the Dartford Tunnel, was agony for me. If I could not even perform these simple tasks, what hope did I have as a javelin thrower?

I suppose what kept me sane was my desire. My superficial

confidence had deserted me, but I somehow kept my inner confidence. I used some psychology to help me through this period, but this was psychology that had been learned simply through my own experiences as a performer, and not from theories or by working with a sports psychologist. As I have said before, we are *always* using psychology, but the key to unlocking the door to the complex world behind it is understanding how to use it, and being able to recognize whether, and where, we have gone wrong.

I had a painkilling injection in July 1993, and although I went into the London Grand Prix at Crystal Palace out of shape, I was extremely motivated to prove to myself and to everyone else that, as an athlete, I was far from finished. To my relief, I finished second behind Zelezny, throwing 85 metres in the process. I immediately thought that if I could produce this, with no preparation, I should enter the World Championships the following month in Stuttgart. One week before they started, at only my second meeting of the whole year, I tore my adductor muscle again.

This was a shattering psychological blow. For the best part of the year, my preparations had been negative. Then, for what turned out to be a very small amount of time, I had seen a light at the end of the tunnel after my surprise display in London. Then, the shutters came down again.

Even though my adductor was damaged again, and my preparation was nonexistent, I still went to the World Championships in a vain attempt to salvage something from a desperate year. I finished fifth, before being elevated to fourth place after the competition's bronze medallist failed a drugs test. Looking back, I have to conclude that, under the circumstances, it was as good a result as I could have expected.

But the Steve Backley of 1990, the young man who was going to sweep up every Gold Medal going in world athletics, seemed like a distant memory. I left Stuttgart in a terribly depressed state. I told myself that, because my preparations had been so poor and my mental state had been appalling, I had been unprofessional. I was on a roller coaster of emotion, running myself down physically, partly as a result of my mental state. Within a week of the World Championships, I developed chickenpox, an illness which often results from being run down.

I think that this was the first time that I actually stopped being a headless chicken and cross-examined myself. It had been very difficult to take. A standard had been set three years earlier, not only by myself, but also by my friends, my family and the athletics world. I was supposed to be winning, not busting my gut to keep finishing outside the medals. Worse still, my sport, or rather the way I was handling my sport, was clearly making me unhealthy.

This was the turning point of my career. I had reached the highest peak in athletics, only to plummet dramatically, but from the winter of 1993–4 my fortunes began to change for the better. I took three months off in order to take my mind off the sport, and gather my strength and my thoughts. I then made a crucial decision.

From this point I became truly professional, paying more attention to my diet and being more in tune with my training. More importantly, I recognized, for the first time, that I should also concentrate on adopting sports psychology. I sat down and, by looking through my training diaries, I began to get a clearer picture of the ups and downs of my performance. I realized that, suddenly, my career was not going according to plan. Events seemed to have speeded up, and the result was that I had less control over my preparation and my performance. It was then that I understood that psychology had both worked for and against me in the past, coinciding, respectively, with my best and worst performances.

One of the first moves I made was to set myself a goal. For some reason, I had always been concerned about throwing the world record; it was something I saw as my personal property. But any athlete will tell you that world record holders will always see someone take away their record, but no one can ever take away winning a major championship Gold Medal.

I set my sights on the 1994 European Championships in Helsinki and, like a blinkered horse, did not allow anything else to get in my way. Of course, during 1992, the focal point of the year was the Olympics; during 1993, it was the World

Championships. But the difference here was that, in 1994, I actually made a conscious decision to concentrate fully on the psychological goal that I had set myself. It meant that I prepared myself in a correct and professional way. I did not try to throw the world record at every meeting. If I had done so, I am sure I would have injured myself again and would once more have started up the cycle of the previous two years.

As the European Championships began, my mind was – for the first time at a major meeting since 1990 – in good shape. I was well rested, and it was not generally expected that I would win. As I mentioned earlier in this chapter, there is always much less pressure when you are the underdog. I also think being written off by people, particularly the press, spurred me on to prove everyone wrong.

Even the game plan worked well. I produced a big throw early on, putting everyone else under immediate pressure. I, therefore, not only manipulated my psychological state, I manipulated everyone else's as well. Of course, I was more than happy with the result. After three years of failure, I had bounced back. What was particularly satisfying was that I recognized how I had used psychology to great effect, not only in theory but, during my training, my preparation and, in the actual competition, in practice.

A week later, still on a high, I travelled to Victoria in Canada, and promptly won the Commonwealth Gold Medal. The opposition was not as tough as in the European Championships, when I faced every top thrower in the world, but it was still crucial for my recovery process to win.

If 1994 was the year in which I wanted to consolidate myself as a javelin thrower, then, in 1995, my aim was to consolidate myself as a winner. I started the year with two aims: to throw as close to 90 metres as possible and, more importantly, to perform as well as I possibly could in the World Championships in Gothenburg. During the season, a couple of Germans suddenly came into the picture, providing even stiffer opposition, but I followed the same route as I had in 1994, resting myself, and focusing on my goals.

I found the experience of winning a Silver Medal both

pleasurable and disappointing. Although Jan Zelezny was the favourite, I still went to Gothenburg to win. To be completely satisfied with second place would be an alien feeling. However, when you consider my previous two performances in the World Championships, the fact that I had been out for so long prior to 1994, the added fact that the competition had become that much tougher, and also that I managed to produce that Silver Medal-winning throw in the last round of the final, the result was extremely satisfying.

This all means that I have established a credible base now in my campaign to become the 1996 Olympic champion. Six years ago, people would have expected this. Three or four years ago, nobody would have placed bets on Steve Backley becoming Olympic champion. Of course, it will be incredibly difficult to win. Jan Zelezny will be the man to beat, and there will be a few others who are also capable of producing a throw big enough to win, but, after too long in the wilderness, I can approach the Games with confidence and total belief in my ability.

I hope my potted sporting biography underlines many of the points I have made about sports psychology. As the psychologist said to Basil Fawlty during an episode of *Fawlty Towers*: 'We have a case here for a whole conference.'

Winning is not necessarily about becoming the Olympic champion. Everybody wins and loses every day. My interest is in how you handle the pressure that you place upon yourself. Having been through it myself, I could relate to the England footballers who missed their penalties during the 1990 World Cup semi-final penalty shoot-out against Germany. I could relate to Bernhard Langer, who faced the ultimate sporting pressure when he had a getable putt to win the 1991 Ryder Cup, and missed. Yet my Olympics, and their World Cup and Ryder Cup, are, in essence, the same as everyday situations you find yourself in, when you allow the mind to take total control.

During the course of this book, I will examine, in much closer detail, where I have gone wrong and where I have gone right, in order to help explain the best ways to utilize your mind. Each chapter will study individual elements of sports psychology, a collection of disciplines, which often cross over into each other's paths. I will begin the chapter with a true story from my own experiences as a top athlete. The purpose of the story will be to show how my mind played an important role in the outcome. I will then move into the theory behind the psychological instance revealed in the story, before examining the practice required to achieve success.

It is an attempt, if you like, not only to communicate my practical experiences, but also to show that I am an average person, from a normal background, who has come to realize that the difference between winning and losing, whether in sport or in life, boils down to a choice that only you can make. Success, certainly in sport, is not necessarily a matter simply of physical predetermination, but one of an internal choice.

I will never think that I have mastered my mind. That would be impossible. I am sure there will be times in the future when negative psychology will work against me again, but at least I have learned, mainly through my mistakes and experiences, how to understand and, at times, how to control my mental state. This does not make me a great teacher, nor a leader that readers of this book should blindly follow to achieve success in life. It simply makes me someone whose eyes have been opened to what can be achieved if you put your mind to it.

This last point is, I feel, the crucial one. You can read books full of theory, and you can be told by people like me how to crack the mental minefield, but only you know your own mind. Different situations produce very different effects, and the end result, whether it is success or failure, ultimately boils down to you and your mind.

The next 10 chapters will therefore help you to make the most of your mind in the way that I, on some occasions, have made use of mine. They will not guarantee anything because only you have the final say in life. But when it comes to the mind, we all start out on a level playing-field. The choice then is up to you.

1. MOTIVATION

··

In psychology, every strand is linked. When you set yourself a goal, for example, it helps to visualize that goal. If you succeed in this, you must ensure that you do not become overexcited, or overaroused, and that you stay relaxed. Throughout the whole cycle, you need to be aware of all the factors, because if you ignore one element, you can quickly find yourself veering off course. But there is still a definable process in sports psychology, which begins with the moment you first think about your ultimate goal, and ends when you have achieved it. Psychologically, the first element everyone needs in order to take the next step forward has to be motivation, because without this crucial factor, no one would never even get going. Before deciding on your objective, you need to have the will or motivation to make the decision, or, as we will later examine, to set yourself your goal. This is why this chapter will focus on motivation.

STORY ···

The following example from my own career not only points out the importance of motivation, but also shows, like all aspects of psychology, how it can work against you if not used in the correct fashion. As you will find out later on in this chapter, motivation is a matter of conscious decision-making. From my personal experience I have found that, by stating my priorities, I have been able to manipulate my motivation to my advantage.

It was early 1993 and I was feeling good. Disappointment about winning 'only' an Olympic Bronze Medal the summer before had been replaced by optimism about the forthcoming season. Surgery on my shoulder, together with the fact that I was the world record holder, meant that I was in a very positive frame of mind.

I remember the day vividly. I took a day off training and went fishing. It was one of those beautiful spring afternoons; I caught four trout, and felt very happy about life. I decided to pay my parents, who lived nearby, a visit, and when I arrived at their house, my mother came out to greet me, and I knew instantly that there was something wrong. She asked me if I had heard the news. What news? I'd been playing music in the car, singing along without a care in the world.

She then told me that Jan Zelezny, my great rival, had just broken my world record. My initial reaction was philosophical. Then came the next sting. He had not only broken my record, he had obliterated it, throwing 95.66 metres, which was over four metres further than my best. In javelin terms, throwing more than four metres further is like running half a second faster in the 100 metres. I could not accept it. I had to watch his throw on video countless times before I finally believed he really had launched the javelin that far.

The news provoked an immediate psychological reaction. One minute I was positive and looking forward to the season in a confident and relaxed manner, the next I realized that I had suddenly become second best by a long way. The laid-back Steve Backley turned into a young man filled with a sense of urgency. I had to get my skates on, and the motivation to get back *my* world record consumed me. All I could think about was throwing the javelin beyond 96 metres.

What I did not accept was that my body, at that time, was just not physically up to the unreasonable and unrealistic task I had set it. My shoulder was not ready for world record-breaking throws. It was rather like someone who has broken his leg deciding that he will not merely be walking in three weeks' time, but running. I should have consolidated, but instead I went for broke. In the competitions leading up to the World

Championships, it was the obsession with regaining my world record that drove me, and not the thought of the biggest title on offer that year.

Looking back, it comes as no surprise that I not only failed even to get close to Zelezny's world record that summer, but that I also failed to win a medal at the 1993 World Championships in Stuttgart. I remember being in a very negative state of mind at the World Championships, and the reason was that the goal I had set myself that season – that of winning back my world record – had not been achieved. I am positive that, had I recaptured the world's best throw, I would have arrived in Stuttgart in an incredibly positive state and might well have won the world title. Instead, I finished a poor fifth, which was improved to fourth after the bronze medallist was disqualified after failing a drugs test.

That day remains so clear in my memory. I remember walking away from the stadium. Don't forget, I had enjoyed the experience of winning, most notably at the 1990 European Championships and Commonwealth Games. I knew that while I was walking away, Zelezny would be sitting in media conferences, talking to television reporters, answering journalists' questions, and generally lapping up the attention that every winner enjoys.

In contrast, I was receiving almost apologetic smiles from people, and awkward 'never mind' words of encouragement. An English girl came up to me and asked for my autograph. My self-esteem was so low at that point, and my disappointment in myself so acute, that I actually asked her why on earth she wanted my autograph. She looked at me as if I was stupid and replied: 'What do you mean, you've just come *fifth* in the World Championships!' My attitude was: Yes, but so what! I should have done so much better. I knew I had the talent and the ability to be the best, so finishing fifth was way below the standard I had set myself.

I can now say that the process towards winning the 1994 European Championships Gold Medal in Helsinki began that same day back in Stuttgart. I remember sitting next to my coach, John Trower, on the bus that took us away from the stadium and back to the athletes' village. I was totally drained and dehydrated, the sweat pouring off me. I told Trower I was never, ever going to let this happen to me again. I had been unprofessional in almost every aspect of my preparation for the World Championships. I was wracked in pain again and realized that my direction had been totally wrong. That bus ride was symbolic for me. I was not only being taken away from the World Championships in Stuttgart, but away from my old approach, and towards the new me. Even as I sat on that bus, as it threaded its way through the busy city streets, I was thinking of Helsinki and the 1994 European Championships.

I flew home the next day. I had no reason nor desire to stay at the World Championships. My bid for the world title was gone, and celebrations were hardly in order. I wanted to leave it all behind me and get on with rebuilding and preparing for what would turn out to be a successful comeback. My determination out of adversity was so great that I decided right then that I would not compete again that summer, but that I would get myself physically – and mentally – sorted out.

On the flight home, my friend and British rival, Mick Hill, whose fourth place had been improved to a Bronze Medal following the drugs scandal at the World Championships, wished me luck for the forthcoming winter training, adding that at least it could not get any worse for me. Within a week I had been laid low with chickenpox but, in my new frame of mind, I read this as my body telling me I was run down, and that all the badness inside me was now coming out.

The crucial decision I came to was that, from that point onwards, I was going to forget about world records, and about being the man who could throw the javelin further than anyone else in history. The problem with records, you see, is that they will always, one day, be beaten. When this happens, your former record is instantly forgotten. The good news about major championships is that nobody can ever take away your Gold Medal. Even during the depressing years of my career, I was still the European and Commonwealth champion. Athletes are remembered for their titles, not their records. From then on, I became focused on winning titles.

World records are very rarely broken in the javelin during major championships. As a javelin thrower, your mental frame is tested so much during competition that the reason for victory can, quite literally, boil down to being in a better mental shape than your competitors. There are possibly six people in the world who are, judging by the distances they have thrown, capable of winning the big titles, but they are not all, necessarily, capable of producing their best efforts when under the pressure of competing in a major championship.

I therefore reasoned that I did not need to keep on pursuing Zelezny's 95 metres record. All that mattered was being fit, and being in as good a physical and mental shape as possible for the day of the European Championships final. I remember winning the first competition of the 1994 summer in Crete with a throw of 85 metres. I had felt good during my training for the season, and I arrived in Crete with an almost natural motivation to throw over 90 metres and threaten that world record. It was as if I was fighting against a motivation that had previously controlled me.

I was disappointed with the distance I had thrown to win the competition, but then I suddenly remembered Stuttgart, the summer before. Suddenly, all that mattered was that I had won the event with a decent throw, and that my body felt fine. That was the key to success at the European Championships, a couple of months later. I went through the summer mainly winning, but occasionally losing competitions, but always seeming to throw around the 85-metre mark. I saw them as all stepping stones to the European Championships. I knew that becoming consistent did not necessarily guarantee that I would win the European Championships, but at least it ensured that I would produce a good throw, which might well be long enough, on the pressure-filled day, to win.

The other factor in the build-up to the European Championships was that, for possibly the first time since I had broken into the world scene, the press were writing me off as a potential gold medallist. After the failure of the 1991 and 1993 World Championships, and the relative disappointment of an Olympic Bronze Medal in 1992, they had clearly decided that I was never going to get back to the highs of 1990. Although it was a relief not to have the added pressure of media expectations on my shoulders, it still hurt my pride.

The game plan for the European Championships final was the familiar one I had used since I had been a teenager in school athletics – throw a big one early. My first effort was okay, but I had made a slight error, and although I found myself leading the competition after the first round, I knew the distance I had achieved was not enough to ensure victory.

It all came together in the second round. I suddenly felt a rush of excitement; by leading the field with a throw that I considered poor, I realized I could quite easily win the title. As soon as the javelin left my hand for my second throw I knew I had won. Throwing the javelin is one of the most popular sports in Finland, and I remember how the crowd of 45,000 screaming Finns erupted as the javelin flew through the air. The distance, 85.20 metres, does not seem huge, but in the difficult climatic conditions, it was very big. I ended up winning the title with a throw that was more than three metres longer than anyone else's in the rest of the field. Although it was the European Championships, the field in question represented the best javelin throwers in the world.

I entered the European Championships ranked only tenth in the world on distance thrown during the 1993 season, but ended it as both the European and Commonwealth champion. Although quite a few throwers had achieved longer distances that year, my average throw placed me second in the world. What a difference from the summer before!

THEORY ....

So how do people become motivated, and what shape does motivation take? Here are some of my theories on what explains motivation. Motivated people can be divided up into two categories:

• Those who want to win

• Those who don't want to lose

In other words, is the golfer who faces a 6-foot putt for $500,000 thinking about the money and glory he will gain, or the money he will lose and the ridicule he will face if he misses? When you train a dog in a non-sporting scenario, should you reward it for good behaviour, or punish it for bad behaviour?

Every successful sportsperson, in whatever field, faces the same consequences. Winning can mean acceptance and recognition by family and friends, coaches, colleagues and spectators. Winning will almost certainly result in fame through increased exposure in the broadcast and written media, and wealth, through the chance to sign lucrative contracts, endorse products, gain promotions and attain bonuses to existing arrangements. The list is endless.

Failure makes for a totally contrasting picture. It can mean a loss of respect, a lack of acceptance by everyone, and even ridicule from the media. Fame, wealth and self-esteem all go flying out of the window. If anyone knows both sides, it is me!

But both these thoughts are based on the theory of *want*. The question you are asking yourself is: How much do I *want* it? The key to this is deciding what makes you tick? What is it that gets you going? For many, achievment is intensified when there is a reward, whether it be a Gold Medal, or simply a drink in the bar after a training session. Structuring reward schemes around training and competition can therefore have the desired effect of increasing your motivation by, for example, presenting yourself with a reward after a training session.

In sport, then, the person who continually strives to avoid being beaten places him or herself under a great deal more pressure than the person who aims to win. It is these external factors that can increase the *intensity* of motivation. Intensity is a very important ingredient of motivation, but it does not necessarily guarantee that you point yourself in the right direction. In fact, if you have misdirected your motivation, your level of intensity can only help to work against you.

Short term, the external factors listed above can help to produce an instant result. For example, when I have entered the last round of the javelin knowing that I am lying out of the medal placings and in need of a big throw, the sense of impending doom has sometimes been enough to stimulate adrenaline to a level that has produced a performance better than my previous attempts.

However, long term – which is what the motivation to succeed, whatever goal you may be pursuing, is ultimately concerned with – you can achieve a great deal more contentment by motivating yourself with the knowledge that you have found self-control and security, rather than continually seeking the approval of others.

There is, in a sense, a positive cycle that can be drawn up here to illustrate my point. Positive self-image equals a positive attitude. This, in turn, will create positive expectations, which will result in a positive display and an increase in performance. What does a good result normally mean? A positive self-image.

Therefore, motivation and a positive self-image are inexorably linked. They feed off each other and are crucial in the first psychological steps towards eventual success. In a sporting sense, this is very applicable to an athlete's out-of-season training, during the often cold and wet winter months. Every athlete will tell you that, when the sleet is falling out of the sky, and it is dark, you need to be motivated to apply yourself correctly. But the same can be said of any situation in life in which you face a daunting task. By adopting my recommendation of self-approval, you should throw yourself into your sport, or whatever you are doing, with a great deal more vigour, purpose and confidence.

Motivation can therefore be described as the direction and intensification of effort. You cannot benefit from motivation if you get just one of these areas right. Correct direction still needs intensity, but intensity will only create more problems for you if the direction is wrong. The other important point to reinforce here is that while all these rules are general, the definition of intensity and direction boils down to you. In other words, the level of intensity and the specific direction I need for motivation and, in the longer term, for success, may well be completely different to your needs.

There are plenty of sporting examples to back this up. When you consider someone like Bernhard Langer, you often wonder how he can keep himself motivated to keep on winning tournaments. It certainly cannot be for the money, so it must be because he still wants to win. It is the competitive nature of the man still to be the best, even if his sport has already provided him with a lifestyle and record of achievement he aimed for when he started to play golf.

In contrast, someone like Chris Eubank has always made it clear that his motivation to keep on boxing, until his retirement in October 1995, was down to earning money. The thought of big pay days kept him going through the rigours of one of the toughest and most gruelling sports imaginable. On a lower level, what is it that motivates the club performer? Money is rarely the issue here. Is it for the pure enjoyment, or social acceptance, perhaps? Maybe, but where does this desire to win come from? What difference does winning make to a club performer? This is where our inherent motivation, which exists in some more than in others, makes us want to be better than our opponents. Everyone's motivation differs slightly, but the common goal is that of aspiring to greater achievement in life. Sport gives us a vehicle to implement this and, in some instances, actually to achieve success, which can reflect back into our lifestyle.

Wanting to better your existing lifestyle is often a fundamental motivation, which is why many people who are successful often come from a background of some adversity. But even though a disadvantaged beginning in life should produce a natural motivation, I do not see motivation as something that exists within certain people only. Motivation is a state of mind, and as this book will repeatedly state, a mind is something that we all possess. The trick is to get as much out of it as possible. Those who succeed do not necessarily possess 'better' minds. They have just decided to utilize and direct the mind.

SUMMARY

What, then, is the relevance of my story to the theories of motivation? The answer is simple: nobody could have doubted my intensity of motivation during 1993, but it is now obvious to me that my direction was way off course, and it was this intense but misdirected motivation that resulted in a disastrous summer.

By motivating myself into an attempt to win back my world record, a goal that was clearly beyond my means at that time, my motivation was poorly structured, poorly managed and, therefore, poorly directed. Even though I still wanted to win the world title, and had entered the competition believing, as every sportsperson has to, that I could win, the reality was that I had, mentally, given myself little chance of becoming world champion. I am not saying that if things had been different I would have definitely won the 1993 World Championships Gold Medal. There are always other physical factors that are difficult to take account of. But if I had been properly motivated, at least I would have given myself a better chance of success.

The decisions made on that bus journey away from Stuttgart's Necker Stadium did not centre on my lack of motivation, but on my motivation's lack of correct direction. I had performed well in the major championships in 1989 and 1990, and knew that this was the way I should be directing myself. I also knew – and this is a golden rule for everyone – that I must set myself realistic, attainable goals, because if, as Zelezny's world record in 1993 proved, the goal is unattainable, subsequent failure to meet the targets set can have disastrous consequences.

The difference between me now and then is that I no longer see the summer of 1993 as the season in which I failed to get back my world record, but as the time I failed to win the World Championships. Given a choice between throwing 90 metres and finishing third, or producing a throw of 80 metres and winning, I will now plump for the latter proposition every time.

My success the following summer at the Helsinki European Championships was a direct result of my realization that I had made, mentally and physically, fundamental mistakes. This is not any great admission of failure. We all make mistakes; the trick is to learn from them. As Nick Faldo once said: 'All the most successful people in sport have failed more often than they have succeeded. But when they fail, they learn.' I can certainly state that my experiences of losing between 1991 and 1993 played a major part in my subsequent experiences of 'winning' in 1994–5.

At a more basic level, why is it that if you lose the first set in a tennis match, or the first game at squash, you always seem to try harder afterwards? You should have been motivated when you first stepped up on the tennis or squash court, yet the experience of losing initially creates a new level of intensity in your motivation to win. Again, the direction comes into this analogy, because trying harder does not necessarily mean that you are going to improve. You need to recognize why you lost in the first place, direct your motivation towards those areas you identify with future success, and then try harder. Trying harder, however, does not necessarily guarantee a better outcome. This will be examined in the chapter concentrating on 'Arousal' later in the book.

Having established the right direction, you then need to acquire intensity in order to ensure that you never waver in your pursuit of your ultimate goal. Intensity can be a natural, in-bred ingredient, but it can also be nurtured and developed from experience. Bruce Lee, considered by many to be the greatest exponent of martial arts, was a small and skinny child, who was continually bullied and beaten up at school. He decided enough was enough and decided to learn how to defend himself. His motivation was that he decided to do something about the situation.

Reward can also be used to increase the intensity of motivation. I am sure that most of you who play golf, as I do, like to enjoy a round with a friend, have a laugh, and look at the birds and the trees without worrying too much about the final outcome. But as soon as someone announces that the next hole is for £5, there is a sudden increase in direct motivation to play a series of better shots.

A sports psychologist called Alan Fine once told me a true

story about a well-known golfer. The golfer was struggling with his technique and concentration. He had the ability but not, it seemed, the right motivation to do something about his failings. Fine ordered him to write out a cheque to a charity for £1,000. The golfer agreed that if he did not carry out Fine's suggested adjustments to his game, Fine would send the cheque off to the charity. If, however, the golfer learned to concentrate, and therefore improved his technique, Fine would return the cheque.

The golfer entered the next tournament with this financial threat hanging over him, and won! Fine had found a way to motivate this golfer. The golfer's motivation had not only found the right, personal direction, but was also intense enough to prove decisive. As a result, the golfer's concentration and technique were spot on. By the way, in case you are wondering, Fine then reasoned that, because the golfer had won a large amount of money, he could afford to send £1,000 to charity in any case.

Even though my preparation for the 1994 European Championships had been good, there was still a danger that it could have gone wrong on the actual day of the final. I had a slight problem with my Achilles heel, and I was being strapped up just before the start of the competition. This was potentially a mental problem; it certainly had been in the past. But, as I lay on the bed being strapped up, I took myself back in time to the previous year at the Stuttgart World Championships, and I remembered how down and humiliated I felt as I walked away from the stadium. I then thought about the period of time since that depressing day. I actually spent five minutes reliving the past 12 months of training and rebuilding myself to the position I found myself in on the day of the 1994 European Championships final. After this mental exercise, I jumped up and told myself that now was my chance to do something about the previous year's disappointment. So, although I had already been through this process in order to motivate myself for the season's preparation, I then motivated myself for an immediate performance in the final.

The ultimate intensity can be revealed in latent, previously undiscovered strength. Everyone has heard the story of the mother who sees her child knocked down and trapped under a car. She rushes over, lifts the car up and pulls the child out from under the car.

If she has that kind of strength, why doesn't she show it all the time? The answer is simple: the intense level of motivation demonstrated here is triggered by the circumstances, and how often is she in a situation comparable to seeing her own child in such obvious danger? As morbid a story as it reads, it does underline the fact that we possess an inner strength, mental and physical, which we can tap into, but which we never fully use.

We often underestimate the level of motivation we could acquire. Examples such as the above prove that we have much more potential than we ever fulfil. The trick, in sporting competition, and in life, is to try to use that latent but nevertheless potential motivation. Nobody can do this, of course, at least not consistently. All you can do is to try to get as close as you can, as often as possible. The trick is, therefore, to maximize the intensity of your motivation. At the same time, you should be maintaining the correct direction by following your attention, so that an increase in intensity will be immediately reflected in your performance.

I have often found that when there seems to be a lack of motivation to achieve, by focusing purely on the element of winning for its own sake, as opposed to worrying about technical positions, the views of others, the possible rewards, or whatever, there is an immediate return to what is the essence of competition: trying to win. My own experience of this was during a stage of the 1994 season, in which I had been hampered by injury. At the time, I almost felt as if I couldn't be bothered to compete. By dispelling my internal doubts, simply through enjoying the competition itself, I was able to improve my performance sufficiently to take me from third to first place.

The chances are that you are a motivated person, without even properly realizing it. It has probably been decided at a subconscious level. You now have to make a conscious decision to be motivated. The fact that you are even reading this book is a good sign. It represents immediate proof of motivation. A well-motivated person will then always set out very clear and established goals. You must have motivation in order to set yourself goals, but once these goals are established, then they, in turn, will help direct your motivation.

2. GOAL-SETTING

....

Having an understanding of how your motivation is made up will, hopefully, give you an opportunity to direct it. It is a crucial step to assume, at this stage, that your motivation to win is now in place. That's the first hurdle cleared. You really want to succeed, and you're determined to do something about it. But succeed in what? Just what exactly are you trying to achieve?

Well, the answer is, of course, your goal, whatever it may be, whether in sport or in life. Your goal is your ultimate objective, the climax of the psychological process you have adopted in order to get as close as you can to achieving your potential. In order to attain your goal, first you have to decide what you are really aiming for, and then go for it. In the course of pursuing this ultimate goal, you also need to set yourself preliminary goals along the way to ensure that you stay on the right track. This chapter, therefore, concentrates on goal-setting.

STORY ....

This personal example shows how important it is to set yourself, not only a long-term goal, but preliminary goals along the way. You must also be prepared to be flexible in your goal-setting.

The summer of 1995 proved, ultimately, to be a great success, although not in the way I had imagined. Preparations for the season began almost as soon as I had finished the 1994 season; I was feeling high after my Gold Medals in the European Championships and Commonwealth Games. The goal that year had been merely to consolidate my position as a world-class javelin thrower. After the previous three years of relative failure, I would have been happy to have survived the season, free of injury, and with a few good results under my belt.

The goals for 1995 were to improve my distances and win the World Championships in Gothenburg. By the time the World Championships came, I had enjoyed an injury-free and modestly successful season – nothing spectacular, but an improvement in distance, some success and a mind totally focused on the only athletics meeting that really mattered.

The night before the qualifying round of the World Championships javelin competition, I remember adopting an extremely professional attitude as I began my last-minute preparations. My coach, John Trower, who had been out in Sweden for a few days before, had given me a clear picture of the place, the stadium and the athletes' village. On hearing that the village was noisy at night, I packed my ear-plugs in order to gain a good night's sleep before the early morning qualifying round.

Before going to bed, I used my personal stereo to help me concentrate on the next day, and also to visualize the goal I had set myself. This was: to qualify with my first throw, which would not only work on the minds of my opponents, it would also give me more rest and make me feel extremely good for the final. The qualifying mark was 82 metres, which I knew I could produce, providing I approached it as if it was the final. My experiences from the disastrous 1991 World Championships in Tokyo had taught me the harsh lessons of being complacent. Then again, I had qualified for the final of the European Championships in 1994 with my first and only throw. I had set myself a preliminary goal and achieved it, which left me with a tremendous feeling of success.

At last the morning came, the morning when I would start my campaign finally to win a global title, or at least do a lot better than I had in my one Olympic appearance, and two World Championship performances. As I walked over to the breakfast hall in the athletes' village, I started to daydream about standing in the middle of the rostrum. I could hear 'God Save the Queen', and I saw the Union Jack fluttering high above the other flags. I then thought about what I would say to the media, what my victorious homecoming would be like, and how it would feel the next day to wake up as the world champion. Fortunately, before I became too carried away, I snapped out of this 'dream session' and got on with the day's work.

Everything went to plan. I qualified with my first throw, recording a distance of 83 metres, from a good four metres behind the line to avoid any possibility of faulting. It was a very satisfying moment – taking my boots and vest off, and packing them in my bag, while Jan Zelezny was watching, still needing to qualify and set the required mark. I had beaten him the year before in the European Championships, and the message this time was: 'I'm in control.' Or so I thought.

Funnily enough, it had a reverse affect. Far from daunting Zelezny, it seemed to spur him on, and he went on to throw 90 metres in qualifying. This did not bother me, though. I had achieved my goal, and I understood from mistakes in previous years that I should not concentrate on Zelezny but on my own performance. I did, however, allow myself the small reward of watching the second pool of throwers trying to qualify. I sat up in the stands, with the rest of the first pool of throwers, watching them sweat it out in their attempts to make the final. The fact that I had attained an automatic qualification filled me with a sense of confidence and relaxation, and I could now allow myself to focus on the final.

Like before, I realized that the best way to win the world title was to produce a big throw early in the competition. I was looking for a throw close to 90 metres in the first or second round. If Jan Zelezny has a weakness, it is that sometimes a big, early throw from one of his main opponents can blow his mind. I knew that I needed to produce early, because he would otherwise pull off one of his 90-metre-plus throws. I then began to work out how I could achieve this. After all, it would be all or nothing in the first couple of rounds. It would mean a fast run-up and a throw that had gained a lot of height.

The qualifying day ended and I had every reason to be in a confident mood. All season I had been achieving my preliminary goals on the way to my main aim of winning the world title. I had thrown further than I had done in the past three years, and had trained long and hard, motivated by the fact that I desperately wanted a global Gold Medal. The next night, the night before the final, a disco boomed out of the athletes' village. It would have been impossible to have slept properly, so my British team-mate Mick Hill, who had also qualified for the final, and I went to one of my sponsors, Asics, who found us a quiet hotel five miles away. We had a good feed, high in carbohydrate, an early night and a deep sleep.

The following day, the big day as far as I was concerned, I felt in tune, switched on and motivated as I walked up to the warm-up track beside the Ullevi stadium in Gothenburg. Everything was still going to plan. I saw Zelezny's camp and remember making a point of jogging past, puffing my chest out and lifting myself a little higher, as if to say 'I'm ready and I'm in shape'. This may seem a little childish, perhaps, but it was carried out in such a way as to make Zelezny believe that while I felt good, I wasn't even thinking about his challenge. Of course, I was only too aware that he would probably turn out to be my stiffest opponent, but I wanted him to think that I was not wasting any time worrying about him.

During the warm-up throws in the stadium, I purposefully stayed in second gear, just easing the javelins into the air. One thing I have learned from Zelezny is that you should never make the mistake, as many javelin throwers do, of having a competition in the warm-up, before the real competition begins. If you watch Zelezny in warm-up, he only throws 30 or 40 metres. He knows that the actual competition is the time to produce the big one for real. In other words, save your best effort for when it really matters.

Throughout this period, I reminded myself, over and over again, of the various goals I had set myself for this moment. Then it was time. Warming-up and preparing is rather like the night before Christmas. The excitement is in the build-up. Being led out into the middle of the stadium for the actual competition is like Christmas Day. It's finally come and now it's time to open the parcels and gifts. At last I could afford to think about the present. As the quote says: 'We spend half our lives worrying about what's going to happen in the future, and the other half forgetting what we've done in the past. If you paid more attention to what you're doing right now you wouldn't have to think of either the past or the future.'

As I ran in to deliver my first throw I felt my legs go wobbly through nervous energy. When you produce the perfect throw, you don't actually get to see the javelin, but I could see the whole of one side of the javelin, which meant that it was flying off sideways. I threw an extremely disappointing 81 metres. My immediate reaction was annoyance that this was the first goal I had set myself that had not gone to plan in the World Championships. I allayed my initial panic by reminding myself that I still had five throws in the final, and that I would simply still produce the 'big one' in the second round early enough to prey on my opponents' minds. My next step was to assess my first-round throw, identifying any mistakes and, by focusing on the correct process goal and then visualizing this particular process, prepare for the second round.

This, however, is where the plan went even further astray. A young German called Boris Henry produced 85 metres with his first-round throw. This had an immediate effect on me. I was like a boxer trying to throw a big punch, but instead, I was being hit first. I was so much on the offensive that I had left my defence totally open. After three rounds, I was lying in sixth place, after three very average throws. I already knew that unless I acted quickly, another World Championships would end in disaster, when Zelezny suddenly produced an 88-metre throw to take the lead.

In the space of fifteen minutes, in the time it takes for all the others to throw, I set myself a new range of goals. I realized that my technique had gone astray, but that I still had time to get back into the medals. The fact that Zelezny had thrown 88 metres was irrelevant. In the past, in the 1992 Olympics for instance, this would have affected me, but not any more. He could have thrown 100 metres that day. The point was that I needed to focus on maximizing my own potential, regardless of Zelezny or anybody else.

I worked out that by slowing down and simplifying my run-up and throw I would improve. My fourth-round effort of 83 metres pulled me up into fourth place, but that was not good enough. I could sense another disaster looming. I then made another reassessment of my goals, almost threw away the structured approach I had adopted, and decided just to run in and throw the damn thing. I knew my fifth throw was good as soon as the javelin left my hand. You always know if it's a good one or not within a split second of delivery and follow-through. It soared way into the sky before landing on 86 metres. In the corner of my eye, I saw the official wave the red flag, which denoted that my foot had just stepped over the line. Complete disaster! I had finally produced a world-class throw, only to disqualify myself. Now I had just one throw left to save the season. The previous throw did, however, give me the confidence to remind myself of what I was capable of. I could therefore dispel many of the doubts that were in my mind.

I am sure that I would not have been able to have handled such a situation in the past. My whole season would have died if I had remained even in fourth place. My success in the European Championships and Commonwealth Games the previous summer would have been severely dampened by this setback. It might have been back to square one.

Fortunately, a maturer psychological approach made me realize that the fifth round had simply to be reproduced – with one exception, just making sure my foot stayed within the allowed area. At last it went to plan. My last throw, in the sixth round of the final, produced a distance of 86.30 metres. It was not enough to beat Zelezny, but good enough to overtake Henry and win the Silver Medal.

I rate that performance as my best yet in international athletics. That may sound a little odd, bearing in mind that I have won Gold Medals in other major championships, and that my goal for 1995 was to become world champion, not to finish second behind my main rival, Jan Zelezny. But it is how I came second that pleases me so much.

I had put into practice what I had learned from previous experiences. Very little went to plan, but I was able to fight back and achieve something after all. I feel that says a lot more about me than if I had recorded the throw early on and remained in second place throughout the competition. To use a boxing analogy, it was rather like the Nigel Benn-versus-Gerald McClellan fight, which ended so tragically. In that fight, McClellan was the favourite, and when he decked Benn in the first round, it looked as if it was all over. But Benn somehow clawed his way back into the fight to come out on top. As a result, he got more respect as a person and as a boxer, because he showed the necessary mental aptitude to win against the odds.

I think my World Championships Silver Medal underlines the significant difference between championships and throwing world records. The world record says that, physically, you're great. But it doesn't test your mental capability. The year before, at the 1994 European Championships, everything had gone to plan, and I beat everyone to win. This time, however, little went to plan on the most important day, but I was still able to readjust, reassess and, eventually, to turn things around and record a successful outcome. That is why the Silver Medal is so satisfying.

THEORY ....

In our daily lives and on the sports field, it is very important to be able to identify what our ambition adds up to. It is human nature to want to set goals and to try to work towards them. Without a goal, a person could be said to be unfocused, or just drifting. With a goal, the same person can concentrate that energy and direct it towards a purpose.

There is, however, a great deal more to goal-setting than merely deciding on what it is that you are ultimately trying to achieve. In basic terms, goal-setting can be departmentalized into three main groups, which all work together in your quest for success. Let's look at, for example, my goals for the 1996 season.

My outcome goal is to win a Gold Medal and become

Olympic champion in Atlanta. The outcome goal needs to be identified and addressed first. Even though, by its very nature, it is your final goal, and therefore comes last in a series of events, you actually need to determine your goal-setting in a reverse order. After all, how can you possibly aim for anything, if you do not have an ultimate goal?

Having identified your outcome goal, you must then put it to one side because you need to look at your performance goal. In other words, you must look at and examine the best ways to produce a performance good enough to create your outcome goal – in my case, to win the Olympics; in your case, perhaps, to win your club tennis cup, or to gain promotion in the office. If I am to win the Olympics, I need to perform consistently throughout the season, regularly recording throws around the 90-metre mark, which would signify a consistent improvement of around three metres.

You then need to take the next step, which, once recognized, becomes your first move towards achieving your ultimate intention. You therefore need to address your process goal. Your performance goal needs to be broken down into technical and intrinsic parts that will help create the performance. In other words, the process goal is aimed at giving you the best chance of producing a performance good enough to realize your outcome goal. The process by which I will find the performance to produce that extra 3 metres will partly involve a technique for improving my footwork, which has been affected by a string of injuries over the years, and also making some technical changes that I feel are necessary, and which have been lacking in the past.

So, identify your final outcome goal, decide on your performance goal, and then start off with the process goal required to set the whole ball rolling. A tennis analogy by the American sports psychologist, W. Timothy Gallwey, explains this process in a different light, but one that we should be aware of when setting goals. When he is coaching, he explains to his pupils that they should try to put aside thoughts about hitting a shot hard, or with topspin, because these are outcome goals. He suggests that they should take the procedure down to process, which in tennis terms is all about timing. He therefore tells his pupils to say 'bounce' as the ball bounces, and 'hit' as they hit the ball back over the net. By doing this, they are concentrating on the process, not the outcome, which is how to win the game. After an hour of this, the pupil's timing is so good that each shot will be a good one. The pupil is not thinking about where the ball may land – the future – but just about hitting the ball as the process takes place – the present. But by doing so, he or she sets up a better chance of eventual success.

Having established the subdivisions of goal-setting, we now have to look into long-term and short-term goals. Both still possess outcome, performance and process goals, but the short-term goals usually provide stepping stones for the eventual

THE WAGON WHEEL

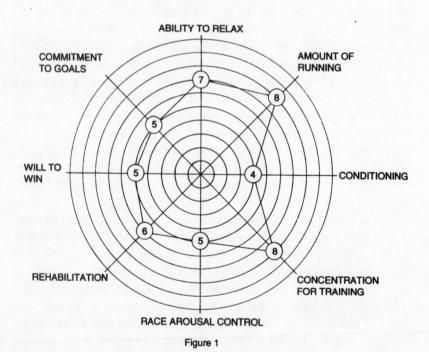

Figure 1

achievement of their longer-term partners.

The only way we can have any kind of direction in life is to have long-term goals. I find the best way to address these goals is to use a scheme introduced to me by Brian Miller, who has worked with me on an individual basis, and also for the British Olympic Association. As the graphic shows *(figure 1)*, the circle, or wagon wheel, depicts your long-term goal. You then identify the top eight factors that you think will play the biggest part in your preparations to achieve your outcome goal. In a sporting sense, I could choose various physical goals (work harder on my strength, flexibility, suppleness, etc.), technical and mental goals (achieve greater distance by better timing and delivery), tactical, strategy and professional goals (early nights, plenty of rest, no damage to the body through work or play). You then number each of the eight 'spokes' of the wheel between zero and ten, depending on how good you are at each of the eight disciplines.

If you are completely honest with yourself, the chances are that you will achieve a higher score in some disciplines and a lower one in others. It will create an extremely unusual pear shape on the wheel. Your job, ultimately, is to produce not only a circle inside this wheel, but as large a circle as possible. In other words, if you can score eight, nine or even ten in all areas, you will produce a large and consistently round shape. The bigger and rounder the circle, the better a performer you are becoming.

The point of this is also to underline the fact that while most people measure their success by means of comparison to others, they should be concentrating on maximizing their own potential. Remember, you should not be trying to be good at the unusual, but concentrating instead on doing the commonplace unusually well. Constant assessment is the key here. Try the wagon wheel process on a weekly basis so that you can measure your improvement. If all goes well, your circle will not only expand, but also form a rounder shape. If any of the components begin to slide in the wrong direction, thus making the circle more irregular, then you must pay extra attention to that weakness. By doing this, you will never waste any time training yourself at disciplines that are unnecessary and, ultimately, ineffective in moving you closer to your outcome goal.

If you use the wagon wheel theory, you will be able to structure your long- term goals. If you don't, then that long-term goal could well seem too far away, and requiring so much work that it feels unattainable. If you work in an office and your outcome goal is to become managing director of the company, you don't just work towards that position, you set yourself intermediate goals along the way in the process towards the final outcome. You first become a regional manager, a national manager, a chief executive, or whatever, and these should all be construed as short-term goals, which, in turn, should be broken down into daily process goals, such as delivering a good sales presentation, or even being on time for work. By adopting this method, then you are guaranteed more chance of succeeding in your short-term goals, which will keep you confident and eager, on the road towards your outcome goal. If you just set yourself the outcome goal and leave it at that, it may well take you too long a time to succeed, which, in turn, could lead to disillusionment and subsequent failure.

You should never lose sight of your outcome goal, of course, but it should not be at the forefront of your mind, at least not while you are concentrating on achieving the stepping stone, short-term goals. It is therefore crucial to recognize your weaknesses and not only work on them on a short-term basis, but also to assess them on a regular basis.

SUMMARY ....

Now that you have read the theory part of this chapter, you should be able to recognize the various elements of psychological goal-setting I used both to my advantage and disadvantage during the 1995 World Championships. You will also now be able to identify how my psychological 'wagon wheel' (figure 1) came into use.

Throughout the last-minute build-up to the final, including the all-important qualifying session, everything went according to my structured plan. Making sure of a good night's sleep was part of my professional goal. Hitting the javelin cleanly with my one and only throw in the qualifying round achieved my technical goal. The fact that I qualified with my first effort secured my tactical goal. With qualification guaranteed, I was then prepared to reintroduce my goals as part of the preparation for the final. Remember, it is crucial to keep on assessing the goals you have set yourself. Although, of course, my outcome goal – to become world champion – remained the same, now that I had qualified, I still had to regroup and work out the process goals specific to the final. I knew exactly what I was up against. The long-term goal was still in sight, but I needed new short-term goals for the day of the final to help achieve my aim.

The daydreaming anecdote in the story also underlined certain important elements. In one sense, it helped, because it made me feel more excited about the World Championships final. This 'aroused' me (arousal is another aspect of sports psychology that we will examine later in the book), yet too much arousal could have been detrimental. As I've said, it is important to stay in the 'mental zone' you have created for yourself, and not suddenly to find yourself drifting, i.e. focused to the point where there are no external distractions.

The point about the actual final is that I began with a certain set of process goals, but I was still able to change them midway through the competition. In previous competitions, I failed to find an answer if the script was suddenly rewritten. I had been stubborn enough before to believe that only my method would work, and I was therefore unable to conjure up a different answer when it became clear that, during that particular competition, my method was not going to produce the desired result. In 1995, however, I had acquired enough mental flexibility to assess whether or not I was still travelling along the right road even though I had already started my journey.

With a greater understanding of psychology, I was able to react in time and put my mind to good use, just when it was threatening to turn against me. It would be unrealistic to think that no problems are going to crop up as a result of being correctly prepared. Nobody should think that problems will suddenly *not* be encountered. It is how we react to these problems that is important.

Funnily enough, I should have found the process relatively easy because, subconsciously, I had already used it to great success six years previously, during the highly successful 1989 season.

I had just won the Europa Cup, my first major international senior title, and arrived in Budapest for the Grand Prix meeting a little tired. My goal was to win the meeting's javelin competition, of course, but once I had produced a reasonable throw early on I mentally switched off. I reasoned that the throw was probably good enough to win, so the focus and intensity on the outcome goal all but disappeared. I actually took my boots off because I did not see me being required to throw again.

Instead, a Russian opponent stepped up in the final round and threw a couple of centimetres further than me. Luckily, I still had my last throw to come. His throw provoked an immediate reaction from me. My motivation was high, and I became extremely focused about beating his effort, an aim that became my outcome goal. The process was just to relax and make sure that my rhythm was correct. The end result was that my final throw was the longest of the night, taking the British and Commonwealth record in the process.

What I achieved that night was all in the subconscious. Maybe that is why it worked so well. The hard part is consciously going through the right mental procedure. The other point about that example is that my natural flair also prevailed that night.

Most people have a flair for something, and while it is important psychologically to structure your process towards your outcome goal, this must not be a substitute for your flair. The secret is to structure your flair. If there is a formula for maximizing your potential, then that is it.

There are many examples of others failing to react. Everything is going to plan one minute, but when the plot changes they fail to react in time. Why is it, for example, that at the end of a major golf tournament, such as the British Open, you often find a relative unknown, or an up-and-coming young golfer at the top of the leader board? I find it amazing that it is almost an inevitability that these golfers are not going to win the whole tournament three days later. Instead, players like Nick Price or Greg Norman, who are lying three strokes behind in seventh place, almost always come through over the remainder of the tournament to win.

Now why is this so? You would think that, given the choice, anyone would like to lead the Open after the first day, but they don't seem capable of holding on to their hard-earned leads. The answer could be this: the early, inexperienced leaders have lost sight of the actual process they should be observing *en route* to their final outcome goal. Just as I was daydreaming on the morning of the World Championships, so these guys could be writing their acceptance speeches in their minds on the evening of the tournament's first day. It is almost human nature to think about the glory of winning, but winning is, and forever will be, the outcome, not the process.

I am not saying that the first day's leader cannot possibly win the whole tournament. Of course he or she can. But they must keep on reminding themselves throughout the four days that, however well they may be faring, they are still in the process, and should be prepared to be flexible enough to change the game plan if necessary. Not many of the golfers who read this will find themselves leading the British Open after the first day, but you can bet that many of them have hit level golf after nine holes, which is a vast improvement on their handicap, only to hit five or six over par on the back nine holes. The eventual round explains why they have such a handicap. Nine out of ten times you will find this to be the case. Your head goes up, you start thinking about that score of 72, and your outcome goal shoves your process goals out of the way and takes centre stage in your mind.

Another example is that of a player leading by two games to nil in a squash match, or being two sets up in a tennis game, then the next stage of the match – which should be the last – suddenly becomes a great deal tougher. The next time you watch Wimbledon, make a point of observing how many five-set matches develop after someone has led by two sets, with the match seemingly all but over.

The answer is down to both players, of course. The one facing defeat, by utilizing the mind, produces a better performance. This is due to motivation, and a reassessment of goals. The one in command says that he or she is just about home. It is very difficult not automatically to relax and ease off the mental and physical gas pedal, but doing so means failing to go the required distance to meet the outcome goal.

The final point to be made here is that, in life, everyone has a choice. Sometimes people allow others to set their goals for them, but in reality, only you are in a true position to decide what your outcome goal should be. This reminds me of an exercise first brought to my notice when I was studying psychology at university – one that I feel is relevant here.

Let us pretend that you find yourself in a situation in which you are asked to score a penalty goal in a game of football. Rather like in a TV game show, you have three choices to make: (a) a £10 reward for scoring from the penalty spot without a goalkeeper facing you between the goalposts; (b) a £100 reward for scoring from the spot with one goalkeeper opposing you; (c) a £1,000 reward for scoring against two goalkeepers standing in goal. Which one would you choose, and why?

Whether you actually succeed in scoring a goal is not a particularly important factor in this model. What is important is discovering whether you can perform close to your optimum, and whether you are prepared to fail.

The chances are that your whole approach and attitude towards choice 'a' would be blasé. You would take the tenner and run. The interpretation of this is that you are not setting your goals high enough for your potential. If you lean towards choice 'b' then it suggests that, on a day-to-day basis, you are setting yourself achievable goals. You think you have a good chance of scoring, but would still be required to make a decent effort to achieve your goal.

If you plump for choice 'c' then you can bet that you will find yourself trying your hardest to succeed. After all, you will need to. A lot of sports people would automatically choose the final proposition because they are prepared to take the risk, knowing that, in attempting the summit, they might fail. I am very ambitious, and I want to win the Olympics. This may require scoring a penalty with five goalkeepers standing in the way, but this is what I have set out to do.

The point is that if you are the sort of person who would plump for 'a' scenario, you should give some thought to attempting 'b'. Likewise, if you would initially attempt example 'b', you should think about raising your sights and trying 'c'. Bear in mind that our goals should remain realistic, but that they should also stretch us enough in order to maximize our potential. Improvement is the idea here.

This is why it is always more beneficial to be stretched to the limit in a game, whether it be golf or tennis, running or table-tennis. You are unlikely to learn much either by hammering your opponent, or by suffering an embarrassing defeat. But if you have either just won, or just lost, after a tremendous struggle, in which both of you have needed to explore the depths of your physical and mental powers, then there is a greater chance of you learning more and, consequently, improving your performance.

Your goals can never be unrealistic, but by being ambitious they will help you get the best out of yourself. If you have structured your goals properly, then you definitely stand a better chance of success. So, to use the penalty analogy, you choose the third situation but, before you actually shoot, you decide who is the worst goalkeeper, choose a particular weak spot, like the bottom left-hand corner, and go for it.

You still have more chance of failing, of course, by picking this final choice, than with the easy, first option, but you also have more chance of applying your optimum effort. I am sure there are people who are perfectly happy to stick with option one, but they will never reach the £1,000 status in life or sport.

If you can say to yourself at the end of your outcome goal that you could have done better, then you have let yourself down, and have sold your mind and your potential short. To reach your goals, whether short or long term, process, preparation or outcome, you need to be able to visualize exactly what you are setting out to do. This discipline provides a vital component to your psychological route to success.

3. VISUALIZATION

....

We are now well and truly into the psychological process needed to achieve success. So far we have addressed some crucial areas and, hopefully, you may now have some idea about motivating yourself, and also setting your sights on the target that you have decided to pursue.

It is important, both at this stage and throughout your route to attaining these goals, that you can clearly identify what you hope will eventually happen. By this, I do not just mean saying to yourself: 'I'm going to take that Olympic title', 'I'm going to win the club tennis tournament', 'I'm going to get that job promotion'. You need to do more than this. In order to know exactly what you are gunning for, you must be able to see, or visualize, almost to the point of physically being there, yourself achieving your outcome goal. If you can visualize correctly, then you should never lose sight of your outcome goal, nor the methods of attaining it.

STORY ....

The following story, split into two parts, highlights what visualization can achieve, both in the immediate, short-term process, and also in the long term. Once again, it shows that if you can really put your mind to it, you can achieve so much more.

It was two weeks before the start of a new athletics summer season, and the winter training had gone really well. I was driving to the athletics track in Dartford for what would be my last serious training session before the season got under way. I was in a confident frame of mind and could clearly see the sort of throw I was going to produce during training. As a result, in my mind, I was moving ahead of the car so that, mentally, I had arrived almost five minutes ahead of myself.

This does not sound terribly safe, I know, but I found myself driving on autopilot, as we all do sometimes when we have things on our mind. As a result, my mind was looking at a split screen, with one part focusing on the track, where I could see myself throwing, and the other part, obviously, still concentrating on the road.

When I arrived at the track everything was how I had pictured it. This was not a huge surprise, bearing in mind that I had trained at this particular venue a hundred times before. Nevertheless, because I was able to visualize the track beforehand, it made me feel more confident and relaxed.

I walked across to the area where I was going to train, remembering as I did so a particularly good session I had enjoyed there before. By the time I had reached the javelin run, I was in the same frame of mind I had been on the day of that quality session.

This time, the training session was going equally well. I'd achieved the technical goals I had set myself for the day, and finished the session with six run-ups to mimic throwing in competition. On the last throw, however, a lapse in concentration resulted in me tripping over my own feet. The javelin 'flew' for about five metres, before sticking into the grass, and I ended up in a heap on the floor.

As I rose to my feet, I was conscious of the fact that I had sprained my ankle. My first reaction was: Oh no, what have I done? All my concentration went, the blinkers came off and, within a few seconds of the accident, my right ankle rose like a Yorkshire pudding. It was only natural that negative thoughts should immediately enter my head.

During my return journey in the car, in my mind I was still back at the track – a reaction to the physical event that had just taken place. I kept telling myself how stupid I had been, kept asking myself what the damage was, and kept thinking about how the injury could have been avoided. I was still analysing all this when, while pulling into my drive, I bumped my car against the garden wall!

After the initial treatment with ice, and momentary elevation, I realized I was going to have to rest at a point only four weeks away from my first big competition. Over the next fortnight, I must have thrown the javelin a thousand times – but all in my mind. I found it difficult not to visualize this without my sprained ankle forcing me to limp, but if I concentrated on the other, unaffected side of my body, I found that the technical process towards throwing became easier.

I must have thrown in every major stadium in the world during this time, and encountered virtually every possible scenario. Consequently, when I was finally able to start throwing the javelin for real again, I carried on from where I had left off a couple of weeks beforehand. Because I had been visual-izing, I was able to get straight back in there. In the past, when I encountered an injury, I had to get over both the physical and mental side effects, but this time I stayed mentally in tune, which meant that I had only to counter the physical elements of the problem.

Now, let's jump ahead. The day of the Olympic final came round very quickly. The alarm went off in my bedroom, and I immediately knew that this was the big day. I was in the best shape of my life, on a day I had worked for, and dreamed about, for the previous four years. I needed the Gold Medal, I wanted the Gold Medal, and I was going to go out and get it.

I was injury free, for once, and feeling both confident and relaxed about the task that lay ahead of me. I remember taking my kit out of my cupboard and arranging it all, making sure I had everything in place, and that my spikes were screwed firmly into my shoes.

Walking across the track to the javelin area inside the stadium, I was very aware of the heat of the afternoon sun. The bag felt heavy, and I could feel my clothes against my skin. I started to jog, just to loosen up and keep myself relaxed. Although I could feel the tension in the atmosphere, I was rising above it all. After a number of technically perfect practice throws, I suddenly stopped, took my shoes off again, and decided enough was enough. I was ready for the final to begin.

When I was taken up to the official call-up room, which all athletes need to visit prior to commencing competition, I was aware of my fellow competitors, and of how tall and strong I felt in comparison. I really believed that I was better prepared than anyone else in the final.

As we all walked out into the centre of the stadium, the atmosphere hit me. Eighty-thousand people were screaming their heads off as a relay final came to an end. As a British athlete, I was immediately aware of the fact that my own country had just won the Gold Medal. The hairs at the back of my neck immediately stood on end just anticipating the excitement of what was about to happen.

I noted that the wind had suddenly changed direction, making the scenario slightly different from the one I had prepared for, but my confidence was so high that I knew I would be able to make the adjustment. I was the first to throw and, once again, the plan was to hit the others with a big, early effort. Everything went right. As soon as the javelin left my hand I knew it was going to be a long throw, but not even I could have imagined that it would beat my personal best and land 92 metres away. As far as I was concerned, that was it. The competition was over, I had won and the Gold Medal was mine. As I walked back, I saw how everyone else's head had dropped.

During the second round, a couple of athletes threw in the high eighties – close enough to remind me that most of the opposition in the final could still be capable of emulating my throw. But I was enjoying the best form of my life, and followed up my first throw with two further efforts just below the mark I had set in the first round.

Jan Zelezny, however, was always capable of coming into the reckoning and, sure enough, in his third-round throw, the javelin landed just centimetres behind my best attempt. This provoked an instant mental – and then physical – response. I was up again, excited and motivated, as a result of Zelezny's sudden challenge. Running even faster before launching my fourth-round throw, the javelin flew over 93 metres, beating the record I had just set in the first round, and enhancing my lead.

Looking around, I saw all heads had now dropped except Zelezny's. His eyes were almost glazed with excitement. He was up for the challenge, and recognized that he was taking part in the greatest head-to-head ever witnessed in the history of the sport.

I knew that Zelezny had enough about him to take me to the wire, so it was not a massive surprise when the Czech athlete produced a mammoth 95.8-metre throw in the fifth round, breaking his own world record and leapfrogging into first place. Despite this setback, I still felt good, but my fifth-round throw – and supposedly my *response* to all this – turned out to be a disaster. It never really took off, stayed flat, and only just crept over the 80-metre mark. As I trudged back, it was Zelezny's turn to be standing tall.

As I prepared for the sixth round, and my last effort, I took a few seconds to take stock of the situation. This had been the greatest javelin competition in history, but I was lying in second place; I hadn't worked as hard as I had, and come all this way, to end up with a Silver Medal. Although I had twice thrown a personal record, it was not enough, and I had to do something about it. Just before I started my run-up, I became aware of two factors. First, the crowd had become silent, watching, with a deathly hush, a small piece of athletics history in the making. Secondly, the wind, which had been swirling around the stadium all afternoon, had suddenly changed direction, creating a more favourable situation for me . . .

> . . . I notice my coach sitting in the first row of the stand closest to where I am standing. He is not saying or even mouthing anything, but just looking at me. His eyes are saying it all. He knows that I can do it, and he believes I'm going to. I suddenly become aware of the heat, the noise, even the smell of the freshly cut grass. I find myself in the most incredible frame of mind.
>
> As I run up nothing else is happening around me. I am completely in the mental zone. It is almost as if two walls have been built either side of my run-up. Nobody, but nobody, can determine

Figure 2

CENTERING

1. Stand comfortably, with your feet shoulder distance apart and your knees slightly flexed.

2. Consciously relax your neck, arm and shoulder muscles. Smile slightly to lessen the tension in your jaw.

3. Concentrate on the movement of your abdominal muscles. Observe your stomach muscles tightening and relaxing.

INHALATION

4. Take a slow, deep breath using the diaphragm. Notice your stomach extending.

5. Consciously maintain the relaxation in your chest and shoulders. Keep chest movement minimal and allow no hunching or raising of the shoulders.

6. Exhale slowly. Let yourself go. As your muscles relax, you will feel yourself get heavier.

EXHALATION

what is about to happen next except me. The blinkers are on, and eighty-thousand people have suddenly disappeared. Suddenly, the dare is on. The dare is to take on Zelezny's challenge and beat the new world record.

As I sprint down the run-up area I feel like a cheetah sprinting across the plains, light, controlled and fast. Every step is taken with meaning so that, when I hurl the javelin out of my hand, it feels like a massive force, a thunderbolt; when, at last, I release the javelin, a huge explosion goes off in my body.

The crowd erupt the moment the javelin hits the ground. I know I have won, and I know I have taken the world record in the process. I even turn round and walk back to my bench before looking at the scoreboard. When the official length comes up – 96.14 metres – the crowd goes berserk for the second time in a minute. It is the ultimate, perfect throw . . .

Conscious of the fact that one must never concentrate on the outcome aspects too much, I lifted my injured ankle from the bench, stood up, and walked out of the sauna. Another good training session had just been completed.

THEORY ....

There is more theory to visualization than almost any other facet of sports psychology. This is because, by its very definition, visualization requires the ultimate use of the mind. The following is a typical visualization session, which should either be read a few times, in order to get the gist, and then performed, or, alternatively, should be transcribed onto an audio cassette. If you choose to do the latter, read this out slowly, in your own voice, possibly while playing some relaxing music on another cassette recorder as you listen to it. Okay? Here goes . . .

Before you can actually visualize properly, you must first be able to 'center' *(figure 2)*. This is a skill that progressively blocks out the unwanted or exterior distractions. You achieve this by centering on your breathing, relaxing and focusing to a point where you are in control. (This also forms part of the chapter on arousal.)

To center yourself, the theory suggests that you sit in an exact, symmetrical position. In other words, your feet astride, and your arms stretched out either side, so that, if you were to draw a line through the middle of your body, each side would be symmetrical to the other. The reason for this is that if you sit with your legs or arms crossed, you are confusing and obstructing the neural pathways from your brain down to your limbs.

Once you have found a symmetrical and comfortable position, and bearing in mind that you could be in this position for 15 minutes, you then concentrate on breathing. Your breathing is the key to focusing on your inner strength and energies. By breathing from the stomach, and therefore concentrating on your body's centre of gravity, with your eyes shut, you should now be ready to begin. Inhale very deeply and exhale very slowly, paying particular attention to your lungs and, more importantly, to the rhythm of your breathing. Try to make each breath you take equal, and, with each breath, relax more and more. After a few minutes of gently relaxing, take a moment to notice how you feel. Notice that you are now in control of everything around you.

Start by concentrating on your arms. Make sure that both arms are turned so that the palm of each hand is facing upwards. Beginning with your right arm and, in particular, the muscles of your upper arm, first see if there is any tension or sensation in that area. There may be a draft blowing, or some tingling. It is important to be aware of this. Then, move your attention up and down your right arm, as if scanning it without actually moving it, taking note of any changes that occur along the way.

Now, shift your attention across to your left arm, and, again, in a very relaxed and controlled manner, move up and down, looking for anything that might cause you to stop and pay attention: notice and acknowledge it, and then move on. You will discover that while you are performing this exercise your concentration will increase with every second that passes.

You then focus on your right leg, again moving up and down with even greater awareness. Just spend the next few minutes continuing this self-assessment, moving up to your torso, and so on. Then, go back to the beginning, using your right arm again, and see if there is any change from your previous assessment. Once you are happy that you are totally in control, allow a feeling of heaviness to enter your arm. Let it become heavier and heavier. Every time you breathe out, notice how heavy you are becoming. Every time you breathe in, notice how it makes your arm lighter again. Light when you breathe in, heavy when you breathe out. Notice how relaxed this makes your arm feel. Then move around your body, making each limb in turn become light and heavy, alternately.

You now feel balanced and centred, and your attention is fully under your control. Slowly, broaden your attention so that you are aware of the room around you. Be aware of any noise in the distance and, eventually, open your eyes and give yourself a good minute or so to come round fully before you get up. You should be feeling relaxed and refreshed.

Take some time to develop this skill of relaxation, because it forms the basis for clear and effective visualization. (Relaxation and the techniques used to become relaxed are examined in greater detail in chapter six). The above is relevant to anyone, whereas what follows is particularly useful to people who play sport. However, there are various elements of the following that can be adopted by anyone.

Always begin the following visualization session with the centring exercise outlined above. Now that you are fully relaxed, you are ready to perform your individual skill. Using the same control and poise with which you moved around your body, move your attention now away from your body, and to the place where you will be training, competing or working. On arriving at the place, notice any changes, sounds, smells, etc. Is it windy? Is it warm? Notice as many points as you can, register them in your thoughts, and then move on.

First, see yourself stretching and warming up in the same way you would if you were physically there. Then, focus your attention internally and notice any tension in any muscles as you begin your warm-up. Notice how well-balanced your body feels. Suddenly, you will be feeling very light, and you will find it easier to move around the area you are working in. You will feel more in control of your movements. Notice how sensitive you are to any changes, and how you seem to be able to respond and adapt very quickly and effectively. Notice how efficient you are in your movements. You are balanced and poised, ready to perform at your best.

Begin your session by putting on any kit you may need to wear. Notice how it feels against your body. Be aware of the sun and the breeze, if you are outdoors, or if inside, the air conditioning. As you make your way towards the first specific movement, see how relaxed and balanced you are, but, at the same time, how poised and awake you feel.

Every day, in every way, you can feel your confidence and your skill improving as you move towards your ultimate goal. When you perform your particular skill you can see yourself being able to perform the skill better than you have ever been able to before. The theory suggests that one of the biggest differences between élite and sub-élite performers is the ability of the former to visualize effectively.

The following spaces should be filled in with your key words, which highlight the specific goals in your mind.

————,————,————,————,————,————.

For example, these are the key words I use in visualizing throwing the javelin:

> position and angle of left foot; left arm; sight lines; hip position.

But my key words for playing golf are:

> slow backswing; still head position; good rhythm in the swing.

If you are playing golf, pay particular attention to how comfortable your stance feels. Begin your visualization exactly as if you were about to start a practice session. Limber up, and focus on external factors, such as the weather, the smell of the grass, how the ball may be lying, and so on, before you take your first swing with the club you are most comfortable with.

Then pay attention to the rhythm and timing of your swing. It will be a useful exercise to progress and visualize every possible scenario, such as hitting the ball out of bounds, out into the rough, chipping and putting in as many different situations as possible. Always focus on performing optimally.

Now, with particular focus on your own key words, go through the skill a number of times in order to identify and reinforce this improved performance. Every time you see yourself going through the movement, your key word skills should improve to the point where you are mastering this skill.

If you happen to be playing tennis or squash, notice how the ball feels in your hand, and how you seem to have better control of the racquet. If, on the other hand, you happen to be running, notice the control and balance in your stride. Whatever your particular skill or event may be, work through this process in a purposefully slow and methodical way, so that you are in control of every movement and always at normal speed.

An important rule throughout this process is that you must always visualize yourself performing your skill to the best of your abilities. Take a good few minutes to see this particular skill, and work through it. When you are happy that you have developed even a small part of you, you can call it a day. Then, slowly become aware again of what is around you, before broadening your awareness so that, eventually, you become fully awake. Open your eyes and look around you, get your bearings again, and stand up.

The visualization session is now completed.

Now, if all the above sounds a little way out, remember the point I made in the introductory chapter. I am a very ordinary guy from the London–Kent borders, with a very average background. By putting my mind to it, I can perform the exercise I have just outlined for you. If I can do it, then so can you. In fact, so can anyone!

Everything should be rehearsed in your mind before you actually put it into practice. But the difference between simple daydreaming and visualization is that the latter is a skill that must be learned. It must incorporate all the senses for it to be totally effective, and therefore the art is to recreate a real-life

By the time I was in my late teens, when this picture was taken in 1986, I had decided that my goal over the next few years was to throw a javelin as far as I possibly could. ALLSPORT

The European Junior Championships, held in Birmingham in 1987, were my first venture into international competition. It was a day of dreadful weather, which, happily, failed to put me off my stride. MARK SHEARMAN

Seb Coe leads Steve Ovett in the 1500 metres final at the Olympic Games, Moscow, 1980. Coe and Ovett were the two athletes who first sparked my ambition to represent my country in the Olympics, even though I was barely in my teens at the time. MARK SHEARMAN

Above: August 1990, and a moment to remember as I celebrate the recapture of my world record at Crystal Palace. MARK SHEARMAN

Left: My great rival Jan Zelezny, the Czech who twice took from me the world record, which I had come to assume was almost mine by right. Only when I realized that it was more important to beat Zelezny in competition than to recapture the record did I get back on level terms with him. ALLSPORT

The culmination of the 1990 season, my *annus mirabilis*: I proudly display my IAAF award as Athlete of the Year. Little did I know what disappointments lay ahead … ALLSPORT

… perhaps the worst moment of my athletic career. At the 1991 World Championships in Tokyo, I failed even to qualify for the competition I had been widely expected to win. ALLSPORT

Golf, even if you don't take it too seriously, is a game that demands intense concentration ... ALLSPORT

Below: ... and a little motivation doesn't come amiss either, as my British rival, Mick Hill (on right) and I found when we played together in New Zealand in 1992. ALLSPORT

The 1993 World Championship in Stuttgart; this was a low point, but from the moment I walked out from the stadium, having come only fifth, I started the process that led to success at Helsinki the following year. MARK SHEARMAN

The World Championships in Helsinki 1994 marked the point when I finally learned that by setting myself one goal and concentrating single-mindedly on achieving it, I could recover the winning form that had for so long eluded me.
MARK SHEARMAN

event in your own living room, or wherever else you may decide to have a visualization training session.

A lot of my training technique derives from copying other people who are, in some areas, technically superior. It therefore does not have to be an image that you have necessarily created yourself. It can quite easily come from another person's standpoint.

There is a group of football coaches, for example, who have created a scheme that, basically, highlights all the skills required in football, and which selects the best exponents of each particular skill. They may pick, for example, the heading ability of Pelé, the dribbling skills of Maradona and the shooting power of Bobby Charlton. None of these great footballers own a copyright over their skills, so you are perfectly entitled to watch, learn and try to go away with a similar ability. You are merely trying to create the ideal picture.

In a nutshell, this is what visualization is all about. In your mind, you can do anything. Piece together all the aspects to create the performance required to win, in whatever you might be doing, and if you can see the end result in your mind, the more likely you are of being able physically to achieve your goal.

For it to become a reality, visualization must be as precise as possible, incorporating every scenario in order to prevent any eventuality becoming a surprise. If a camera, for example, is only 90 per cent in focus, you will not see a clear image; it is the same in visualization. The sharper the image, the sharper the performance.

Research dating back to the 1930s, by the psychologist Jacobson, began to prove that subliminal muscular activity takes places during mental rehearsal. When you sit down and watch a football match, why is it that as someone rises to head the ball into the net, you automatically twitch? Why is it that if you are a passenger in a car, and it is obvious that the driver needs to suddenly brake, you find yourself hitting an imaginary brake? The reason is that, mentally, you are being the other person. You are heading the ball and hitting the brakes. By sensing and visualizing, you are playing that role without physically incorporating the movement.

The sequence of events is actually part of your central nervous system. The brain ensures that we can actually learn a skill essentially by watching it in our mind's eye. We don't necessarily have to perform the actual skill.

Working regularly through this session, with a high level of concentration for a short time, is more constructive than looking through it 10 times a day and being vague. Five minutes every morning and evening should be ample time if you are following the process correctly. Always feel relaxed and confident, and always do this by looking out from within. This will always provide the most intrinsic feedback.

If the action you are visualizing takes very little time to complete, keep on repeating the process, over and over again, until you have perfected the action, initially in your mind, which will then translate it into practice.

The final point to be made in this theory section concerns the use of visualization when it comes to actual competition. There are two areas where this can be put to great use: before the competition, and during the competition.

Every potential outcome has to be visualized so that nothing is left to chance. In a sport where you have more than one attempt, like archery, diving or, indeed, my own event, you should always assess your first attempt, make whatever changes are necessary in your professional, technical and tactical goals, and then visualize this new state of affairs.

By doing this, you almost increase the number of attempts you have, and consequently stand a better chance of achieving the desired performance, and therefore the desired result. I have six throws in up to three hours during a javelin competition. That means that I have over twenty minutes between each throw. This time is put to good use. I run through the psychological process, reassessing my goals, and then visualizing them, so that when it is my time to throw again, I am instantly ready, and switched on.

Somebody who writes should be able to relate to this. Writers may spend a good fifteen minutes trying to work out the best way to start a new chapter. Often, however, once they have started, they are on a roll. If, however, something forces them to stop midway through, they usually have to spend time trying to get back into the mood they had previously created.

So, visualization creates the perfect mental imagery. A good visualization session will mean that you already know exactly how to win.

SUMMARY ....

Somewhere during the second part of my story you will have realized that the details I was relating had not actually happened – yet. At least not physically. The purpose of the story was to show, in the first part, what a powerful hold visualization can have on the mind, and in the second part, what you can achieve in the future, using your mind. I did not even realize that I had bumped my car, for example, on my garden wall until much later after the event. My mind was so taken over by visualization, that not even damaging my car snapped me out of it.

Of course, despite what happened in the second part of the story, I have not yet, physically won the Olympics. But in my mind, I have been through the process of winning that Gold Medal on hundreds of occasions. If you still find it a little difficult to believe what a powerful ally visualization can be, then here are a couple of true examples for you.

Brian Miller once told me a true story about a male 400 metres hurdler whom he asked to visualize running a race in his consulting room. For those of you who do not know, this particular event is extremely tiring to perform. You need to combine great speed with the stamina to get round one lap of a track as quickly as possible. In straightforward sprint events, you need speed, while in middle- and longer-distance events, stamina is the more essential ingredient. But in the 400 metres hurdles, you need both, plus the added strength and technique required to clear the barriers.

At the end of his visualized race, the athlete was disappointed to discover that he was two seconds outside his best time. A good visualization session will be run at a speed exactly the same as your performance. The athlete in question was upset to find himself two seconds outside his best time, as opposed to one-fifth of a second. He decided to try again. After 200 metres of his visualized race, he suddenly started to vomit.

The reason is that no 400 metres hurdler would actually, physically, attempt two back-to-back races. They would need to have a decent break in between each race. The athlete proved that his visualization was so like real life that his mental imagery convinced his body that he was *physically* running two consecutive races. Any athlete would vomit if he or she really ran two races in this manner. His subconscious actually believed the scenario.

The other example involves an experiment I took part in while I was at Loughborough University. Three groups were asked to perform the simple task of putting together a nut, a washer and a bolt. The first group were allowed to practice this for 10 minutes before performing the task for real. The second group had to visualize this exercise for 10 minutes, while the last group did neither.

The eventual results were staggering. Those individuals who had been allowed to practice, put together 32 nuts, washers and bolts in 10 minutes. Those who had been asked to visualize managed 30, while those who did neither could only manage 22. The purpose of this exercise was to prove that, rather than doing nothing, by visualizing you can get extremely close to actual practice. The people who visualized their task asked their brains to process the skill and then organize the events required to carry them out.

Anyone can do this. After all, everyone daydreams. Isn't it the case that when you are daydreaming you have, subconsciously, fallen into an altered state of awareness, even if you are physically performing an everyday act? When you are on the verge of either falling asleep, or waking up, you are actually in the process of centring.

This is why you experience your dreams and nightmares just before you are due to wake up. The reason is that you are in a totally relaxed state of mind. It is while your mind is between being awake and asleep that you can make use of this altered state of awareness. Most of us make use of it by dreaming, but this is also the state of mind centring produces in order to perform a constructive, visualization training session.

The only difference between what we all do – daydreaming – and an actual, conscious process of psychology – visualization – is that, with the latter, we are in control, sticking rigidly to the area we want to focus on.

The writing analogy I referred to earlier is useful. A novelist sits at home in suburbia, but in order to describe a fictional place or event, he or she has to be transported mentally in order to write it. Physically, he or she is in the office, but mentally he or she is in India, the storm at sea, or whatever the book requires. So, the novelist also separates the mind from the body, using visualization. The only difference between a novelist and myself is that, while the novelist translates visualization into words, I translate mine into action.

I am sure, in the past, that you have all tried to turn up on the day and see how your sports match, speech or business venture works out. If you have, I am sure that the outcome was not as good as it might have been. I remember once arriving for a speech I was about to make without any preparation. I allowed other commitments to prevent me from approaching it professionally, believing that I would think of something to say. Instead, I just stumbled all over the place.

It has never happened since. You don't leave anything to chance. It has long been accepted that you must prepare the body for a sporting event. No one turns up for an Olympic final without having undergone an intensive period of training. The mind must be trained equally vigorously.

You have probably gathered by now that goal-setting and visualization are a necessary combination. This is why, for example, when I was visualizing my success at the Olympics, I did not dwell on my poor, fifth-round throw. I simply said that I produced a poor throw, and then went straight on to describing, in far greater detail, my sixth, last and world record-breaking throw. This is because you must only ever visualize success. Obviously, if you visualize failure, it will only help to teach you how to fail more.

You will also have noticed that the story ended rather abruptly with my winning throw. There were no medal ceremonies, nor national anthems, nor Union Jacks fluttering in the wind. This is because if I had visualized all that, I would have been concentrating too much on just my outcome goal – that of winning the Olympic title – and not enough on my process goals, in which I find the means and the method of achieving my outcome goal. It is the process of visualizing every different scenario that prepares us fully. The story outlined at the beginning of this chapter is just one example of how I visualize. It is, however, a typical one. Whatever scenario my visualization takes me through, I have found that a continual focus, paying particular attention to my state of mind and technique, which are the two main factors I am trying to develop, is crucial.

By going over this process repeatedly through visualization, it means that as and when the process towards winning takes place, it is already familiar and, therefore, comfortable ground. Consistency and repetition are vital components of visualization.

All the psychological ingredients discussed are necessary not only to getting started on the path to success, but also right the way through the process. Training and preparation seem, on the face of it, to be more of a physical discipline, but you would be surprised how much the mind comes into this vital part of the route to achieving ambitions and attaining goals.

4. TRAINING AND WARM-UP

....

None of the psychological disciplines addressed so far is of any use to you in achieving your outcome goals unless you undergo the correct training procedure and the crucial warm-up period. On the face of it, these two pre-competition elements appear to be physical disciplines, and should, perhaps, be appearing in a book about physical fitness and preparation for sport.

The truth, however, is that the psychological aspects of training and warm-up are just as important to the final performance as being prepared to suffer physically in order to reach peak condition.

STORY ....

Like all the other areas covered so far in this book, training and warm-up are two different processes, which count, not only in the long term, but also on the actual day of your outcome goal. As this story reveals, if you dismiss the mental importance of training and warm-up, there's only ever going to be one result.

I was 19 in June 1988. By this time, I knew I could go all the way in international athletics, and could not be more motivated as a result. Up until then success had come fairly easily. It seemed to be a simple formula. The more I trained, the further the javelin seemed to fly. I never questioned my ability to prepare and compete, and I never really expected anything ever to go wrong. I'm not exactly old now, but I can look back on those days and recognize a very naïve young man. And why not? I could not do much wrong.

I decided to make the most of what was going to be my final year as a junior athlete. The first major competition of the season was the UK Championships, an event I had always held in high esteem. I was really up for it too, having got down and trained very hard all winter to build up my body. Physically, I was in great shape.

The start of the season seemed to be a continuation from the end of the previous one, when I had recorded my best throw of 78 metres. This time, at the UK Championships, I produced 79.53 metres, my longest-ever throw, and a new, junior world record. It was the perfect beginning to what was going to be a perfect summer.

The problem with that first throw was that I had proved myself immediately. It made me take the foot off the accelerator, both physically and mentally, when it came to my training. As a result, the following month saw five competitions fly past. None of the results was as dramatic as the UK Championships, but I was not concerned.

This slight lapse in concentration then led to a foot problem caused by my unsuccessful attempt to trap a medicine ball. It was one of those silly – and totally avoidable – accidents in training, but it meant two weeks off training while my foot recovered, with the World Junior Championships just three weeks away. Still, this did not bother me. I knew I was the best, and I fully expected to go out there and achieve what I was accustomed to achieving. I had never been to Canada, where the championships were being held, but as far as I was concerned, it was just another athletics track. I did not give the weather or the time difference much thought, and just decided to play it by ear when I finally arrived over there.

At the time, I thought I was paying a great deal of attention to every detail by training hard. I did not seem to understand that the mental side of training was equally important. I would therefore turn up for medicine ball work, circuit training and bounding, without ever fully concentrating on what I was really doing. After all, I was the junior world record holder, and I knew what I was doing.

On the day of the qualification round in the World Junior Championships in Sudbury, I was set the task of throwing 70 metres in order to make it into the final. This did not seem much of a problem to me. But I had underestimated – as in fact I had underestimated having to throw early in the morning, which was new to me.

Consequently, I qualified on my second throw, having failed to make the 70-metre mark after my first effort. It was not a very good idea to take two throws to qualify the day before the most important competition of my career.

At the same time I couldn't help but notice this strapping Russian called Ovchinikov, who made his qualification look easy by recording a first-round throw of 75 metres in a very aggressive and impressive manner.

All of a sudden some doubts began to creep into my mind. This was the first time negative thoughts had ever entered my head, and I didn't seem to have much control over them as they grew to occupy my mind. Where did this Russian guy come from? How come he looked so good? Suddenly, I figured, there was someone who had the potential to beat me, and this came as a great shock to me. Overnight, a heat wave had suddenly swept over this part of the country. It meant that by the time we entered the stadium for the javelin final the next day, the temperature was over 100 degrees Fahrenheit. I therefore changed my warm-up to accommodate this sudden heat, and I remember sitting in the shade under a tree by the side of the thrower's run-up refusing to go through my normal routine. Meanwhile, the others continued and, as I watched them running up, and then retrieving their javelins, I came to the conclusion that they were only doing themselves harm.

It was only before the actual start of the competition that I began to wonder if, by not having completed my usual, full preparation whether, in fact, the others were right, and I had made a mistake. I was beginning to wonder what the potential implications of all this might be, but I had made the decision, and it was too late to go back on it now.

As I entered the stadium for the first time the 20,000 crowd, by far the biggest I had performed in front of, came as another shock. We were all told to sit down by a rather strict official. The javelins were put to one side. None of the competitors was allowed to touch the javelin before the official warm-up, which is an integral part of being attuned. I, like everyone else, like to get a feel for the javelin beforehand, rather like a snooker player with his cue, and the official's authoritarian manner was beginning to irritate me.

We were only allowed two warm-up throws. This was something else I was not used to, and I did not feel properly warmed-up when the actual competition began. I had obviously not done my homework too well and hadn't realized that two throws was the normal official preparation for a major championship. To make matters even worse, I looked across at the javelins, and noticed that my favourite javelin of that time, a yellow model called a Sanvik Champion, the type that I had used with great success, including that world junior record, was not there.

I felt as if my whole world had collapsed around me. I was standing in front of a huge, intimidating crowd, in unbelievable heat, without the comfort of the javelin I always threw. Negative thoughts were escalating at an uncontrollable speed. A few detrimental aspects seemed to be changing my whole outlook for that day. I knew the trap I was falling into, but it was still an easy mistake to make. I realized that some days things can seem like they are just not working for you, while other days they do. Although I was conscious of this fact, I was still unable to prevent this from happening to me.

I became very flustered, and turned to the British team manager for help. He came back, 10 minutes later, and said that he could not do anything, which merely added to my frustration. Eventually, enough people complained to force the officials to appear suddenly with three Sanviks, but by then my blinkers were off.

Midway through the first round, strange distances started to pop up on the electronic measuring devices. Throws that seemed to travel close to 70 metres were measured in the fifties, and vice versa. It threw the whole competition into disarray.

What had happened was that one of the three points of the measuring device, situated high up in the stand, had been knocked accidentally by a technician. It meant that the competition had to be delayed for half an hour while the device was repaired.

When you bear in mind that we had to sit in the searing heat, without being allowed actually to touch the javelins, with the competition under way, it was hardly an ideal situation. Half an hour could have been time well spent, controlling myself and mentally preparing for the task ahead. But all I could think about was the strict official in charge of the throwers.

When we eventually started up again, the whole competition appeared to flash past. It seemed to me that within minutes of putting on my tracksuit after a throw and walking around in order to relax, I was being called up again for the next round. I was letting the competition control me. Such negative thoughts changed the concept of my preparation phase, and this resulted in a lacklustre performance.

As the competition progressed, I found myself in second place to the Russian who had worried me during qualifying. While Ovchinikov appeared to grow in stature, I seemed to shrink, and I was looking at him as the potential winner. I remember looking round at the British team manager, who was staring at me in a way which I could only read as saying: 'Come on Steve, you're supposed to be winning this. What the hell's going wrong?' Of course, this only added to my self-imposed pressure.

By now, I knew that my mind had let me down, but it was too late. It was a very frustrating and annoying experience. As my last throw came round I tried very hard to block out everything that had happened before, in an attempt to beat the Russian's leading throw of 77 metres. But all my frustrations were too vivid for me to shut out everything totally, and I could manage only 75 metres, which took the Silver Medal.

Looking back, I was psychologically naïve, but the biggest fault in what I see as one of the failures of my career, was that I had let my mind wander by not having trained and prepared for what was the most important task of the whole summer.

THEORY ....

Training and warm-up can basically be described as getting
attuned – the process of bringing your mind and body together
in preparation for – in my case – competition. In other aspects of
psychology, such as goal-setting, we try and separate our mind
and body, but in this area we must bring them together again, so
that each communicates with the other in order to act as one.

Every sportsperson will recognize that the warm-up is
essential. But there is a lot more to it than simply warming up
your muscles. Similarly, training is not just about practising and
improving. It is the mental preparation during this period that
determines how we are going to use our body. It all adds up to
getting us ready for the ultimate goal in the competition.

Like the other disciplines, training and warm-up can be both
long and short term. Winter training for an athlete, for example,
is obviously long term, but the sequence of events required to
carry out this training is exactly the same as you will find in the
warm-up one hour before the start of a competition.

Our psychology, both in training and warm-up, is therefore
fundamental to maximizing our energies and focusing on our
ultimate goal. If the preparation is fragmented, so too will the
ultimate performance be. Now, let's first look at training.

In a physical sense, training has three parts. First, to attune
our muscles to the particular task in hand; second, it is the
ability to condition and ultimately to learn the skills factor, and
thereby perform more efficiently. The first part underlines
muscle training, the second highlights skills training. But the
third part of the training process is subtly different from the
other areas. This is the preparatory phase, which is all about
preparing your emotions. There are a lot of methods and vast
differences in training physiologically, and they have been well
documented over the years. They are not really the concern of
this book, except to point out that the physiological training
programme chosen, whatever it is, must then be set up through

the process structured in the goal-setting chapter. It is, after all, extremely easy during the heavy training stage to lose sight of the ultimate goal, so it is therefore important to structure the physical build-up properly.

The second part of training addresses the skill factor. This aspect is closely linked to the previous chapter on visualization, with repetition being the key. Once you have seen your particular task in hand, whether it be dribbling a football, or producing a backhand in a racquet sport, repetition will ultimately determine how well you learn that skill.

The learning process of skill in training is stored both locally to the relevant muscle group and in the brain. Just like your muscle's ability to adapt to a training situation, so your brain and, arguably, your central nervous system have the ability to memorize a movement.

These skills must be performed in a proper fashion. If you are ever practising in a sloppy way, your brain will learn that skill in that way, and will then transfer this memory to your muscle areas. You must have body awareness at all times, and by this I mean having the ability to know, with your eyes shut, exactly where you have placed your hands, feet and so on.

It always amazes me how few people actually possess body awareness. I often find myself coaching 10-, 11- and 12-year-old children. I tell them that when you are throwing a javelin, your hands must be above your shoulder. When you look down the line, only 1 out of 10 actually has his or her hand in the proper place. Yet, if you ask them who thinks their hand is above the shoulder, they all think it is. If your body awareness is good, your ability to copy a particular skill will also be good. You really can put into practice what you see if you can master this.

So how do you know whether you are in a good position without looking at it physically? The answer is by possessing a spacial awareness. In other words, by having the ability to communicate with and coordinate your limbs. This, again, requires repetition. How many times, for example, do you look at your gear stick when you are learning to drive? How many times do you look at it now after, say, 5, 10 or 15 years of driving? The answer to the first question is: all the time; and the answer to the second question is: hardly, ever, if at all. You know exactly where the gear stick is simply through repetition and the knowledge and skill factor that you have acquired in that particular sequence of learning to drive. But what do you do if you have already learned a particular skill incorrectly? A psychologist I have worked with called Dave Collins has a particularly effective antidote to this problem.

Do not deny that you have a problem, In fact, go into a training session with this in mind, making sure also that you have found out what *the* good position or technique should be. Once you have identified the correct and the incorrect, first perform the skill in the wrong way. Observe what you are doing, and remember. I know this sounds like strange advice, but read on!

Then, perform the skill in the right way, making a mental note of what you have done. Just like the wrong way, think it through and remember. Then, return to the incorrect method, before performing the correct version again. Once again, return to the incorrect, before then performing the right way twice. Go back to the wrong way, then return to the right way, this time performing it three times. And so you go on. Bad, good; bad, good, good; bad, good, good, good; bad, good, good, good, good – I think you get my point.

So why perform the wrong way at all? Psychologically, there should be a learning curve in your ability to acquire the new, correct skill, but it is equally important to 'unlearn' your bad habit. It may be that you have been practising the incorrect version for many years, so you cannot just drop it. You need to be able to recognize where you have gone wrong, and then, smoothly and gently, remove it from your mental system.

Traditionalists would argue that you must have pretty good insight to be able to realize that you are taking up a bad position, and then to know what the good position might be. But it is crucial to know your old technique so that when, or if, you fall back into the bad old habits, you can instantly rectify the situation, especially in the early days of correction, when you will probably find yourself falling between the two.

As an example, I know that in order to improve my chances

of winning the Olympic Gold Medal I need to change the position of my left arm when throwing the javelin. At the moment, my arm points in the direction of where the javelin is to be thrown, but I have now worked out, using biomechanics and computer playback, that my arm needs to be pointing across my body, almost at a right angle to the javelin's direction. I will therefore be implementing the exercise Dave Collins has taught me in my preparation for the Olympics.

The third part of training is emotional preparation. This is something I have paid more attention to as I have learned more and improved as an athlete. This can often prove to be a sportsperson's downfall, because without focusing on this area, he or she is leaving a massive gap in training.

The best way to achieve this is, when training, to mimic your competition as closely as possible. Both physically and psychologically, you will achieve a better training session if you can evoke the feeling that, instead of standing in a local field on a rainy February afternoon, you are actually at the Olympic Games, or at your school sports day, or standing up delivering your speech. Whatever the occasion, this emotional concept needs to be seen.

For example, if you are carrying out squats in a weights room, you are performing a closed skill. (For those of you who do not know, a squat is a simple movement in which the weights bar is placed across your back, and you then squat, bending your knees and keeping your back as straight as possible.) It has a beginning, a middle and an end. But if you pretend that you are at the Olympics while carrying out this weights discipline, your motivation, focus and desire to perform well will all increase.

We have already addressed exactly why we do this in the previous chapter on visualization, but, now that we are focusing on preparation, it is important to point out the effect this will have when we come to compete. If you have been training with the Olympics in mind, you will have become used to the emotions in good time before the big day, which should ensure that you do not experience new emotions during competition, which might, otherwise, concern you.

In training, a good exercise is to bring the future into the present in order to give yourself an idea – albeit a diluted one – of the emotions you will later be facing. In a sense, you are allowing your final outcome goal to barge into an area where the process goal should be dominant, but this is only for a short period of time – and one in which you need to initiate a period of good training. Once you have found the right emotions, revert back to your process goals, i.e. how am I going to get myself into a position to win the Olympics?

The warm-up concludes your training and preparation, and also introduces you to competition. It is, if you like, a stepping stone between training and competition and something that links the two. This is a phase that can often let people down because there are many people who leave their best performances on the training field.

The warm-up is all about becoming aware, attuning your attention to the task ahead of you. No matter how well your training has gone, if you fail to attune yourself correctly, then your ability to apply your training will not be focused enough to succeed.

There are various factors you should use to increase your focus during your warm-up: (1) your implements and equipment; (2) your body and your mind; (3) the location; (4) people around you, including your team and work colleagues; (5) your goals; (6) your skills; (7) and your emotions.

Your warm-up should begin as much as two or three days before the event, at least in your mind. Your skills, your goals, and your general mental state must become increasingly focused as the day of competition draws closer. Athletes will begin their physical warm-up an hour and a half before the start of competition, but, before this, they should be attuned to the location and to their emotions.

As the warm-up begins, it is always good to identify key people who can help you focus, and also the implements that will help you attune to the specific task that faces you. It is also imperative to control your emotions, incorporating the correct emotions for the task in hand, which you have repeatedly felt throughout training, and also ensuring that any other, potentially damaging emotions are totally blocked out. If you can get the first emotional aspect right, you should find that there is no room for any other emotional thoughts to enter your head.

A classic example of failing to block out other emotions can be seen in the incident during the 1994 Winter Olympics in Lillehammer that involved the two, controversial ice skaters, Nancy Kerrigan, and Tonya Harding. Kerrigan, if you remember, was attacked and injured prior to the games, but made a spectacular comeback. It is pretty obvious that when it came to Harding's performance, emotions over the Kerrigan case were taken onto the ice rink. She could not handle the situation, performed dismally, broke down and cried. Kerrigan was able to block out conflicting emotions and produce a Silver Medal-winning display.

You cannot forget these type of emotions, but when they could have the potential to affect the outcome, you must be able to leave them outside, wherever you may be performing. This can only be done by foreseeing what any given emotion will actually feel like by repetitively visualizing it to the point where you become relaxed with it.

SUMMARY

Now that we have addressed the theories of training and warm-up, the reasons behind the mistakes I made during the 1988 World Junior Championships' campaign should be a great deal clearer.

Obviously, a Silver Medal in the World Junior Championships is by no means a disgrace, but it still could have been better. For me, athletics is not about 'ifs' and 'buts', so I look back on that event as an important learning experience and one that I have never let happen again, at least not for the same reasons.

The first, and most obvious one, is that while I did everything I possibly could in terms of physical training, I failed to take into account the equally important mental aspects. In fact, I almost consciously pushed this aspect aside because I had never had a problem in this area before, and so I reasoned that I must have been following the correct procedure. What had been good in the past would be good enough for the future – I thought. And that began the rot.

The second error came after I began the whole season by breaking the junior world record at the UK Championships. I had achieved one of my main goals immediately, and then switched off. It is very easy to do this. How many times do you see a football team score first, ease off, and end up losing 3–1? Mistake number three then followed. I allowed myself to go through the motions during the next five competitions because I had switched off. I did not apply the correct mental attitude that the meetings demanded, which, apart from depriving myself of crucial practice and experience, also culminated in the stupid accident with the medicine ball. Over a month passed by in which I simply drifted, and the effects of this poor mental preparation were to be revealed in Canada.

A few fundamental elements went wrong on the day. My initial interpretation was that this was not going to be my day. In other words, I immediately had negative thoughts and a lack of confidence, which are always difficult to combat. How many times have you experienced a day when everything seems to be going wrong and you come to the conclusion that, on some days, this is how it is? Being in touch with reality at this point is obviously the key to overcoming this irrational way of thinking. To do this, we must shift our attention towards the present tense, ignoring the past and all of the negative cues it gives us. We must slowly and surely introduce the future.

The dangers of 'drifting' have already been discussed in the goal-setting chapter. I had achieved my goal, and did not possess the foresight or, to be a little fairer on myself, the psychological nous, to set myself a new goal during the preparatory phase.

The next, in what is becoming a long list of mistakes, was my failure to prepare for the specifics of Canada. A little background research never does anyone any harm before starting to visualize. After all, how can you properly visualize if you do not know what you are supposed to be visualizing? An all-round lack of foresight into what I was letting myself into actually resulted in the worst mental preparation possible.

The fact that it took me two throws to qualify was yet another error. This was not a great tactical goal, and it can be put down to bad preparation and bad training. I should have prepared myself correctly to produce the one throw but, at the same time, I should also have been mentally prepared for the possibility of having to take two throws, and not let it have a negative effect on me.

After all, even if your psychological preparation has been spot on, you are still capable of making a mistake. The point here is that once the mistake had been made, I should have also been prepared for this eventuality. You cannot control adverse weather conditions, or the surprisingly good performance of a rival, but you can guarantee not to act negatively if the unexpected happens. If you can foresee them in your mind, then you will enjoy a positive reaction, which will help to maximize your performance.

An everyday example of this is if you have been invited to a party that – on the face of it – does not sound wonderfully exciting. If you decide that you are simply not going to enjoy it, and therefore go in this frame of mind, the chances are that you won't. However, if you say beforehand – 'Okay, on the face of it the party does not look promising, but if I'm going to go, then I may as well make the most of it and enjoy myself' – then, invariably you find yourself enjoying the party. Instead of dwelling on the negative aspects, such as the people were boring, or the music wasn't much good, or whatever, you return home thinking how much better the party turned out. It was not necessarily better, but because your attitude is positive, you have not let a situation, in which elements are out of your control, affect your performance.

What is especially interesting is the way in which a negative approach can then manifest itself physically. For example, how many times do you find yourself in a situation where you have a long, hard day at work, but feel you should still go for your thrice-weekly jog? If you keep telling yourself you feel tired you often find that once you are out running your whole body feels heavier. But if you decide that you want to do this, because you want to get yourself, or keep yourself, fit, then you just do it.

Suddenly, you don't feel tired, your legs don't feel like tree trunks, and you surprise yourself at how easy the run then becomes. Physically, of course, you are no different, but you have made your physical performance a great deal better by mentally preparing yourself in the correct manner.

This is crucial for someone like myself in my preparations for the Olympics. I have to *want* to train hard, carry out circuit training, which, deep down, I dislike, and go running in all weather conditions. I know that either the others are doing it, which means I have to, or they are not, which means that I will give myself the edge. Either way, it has to be done, if I want to give myself the likeliest chance of winning a Gold Medal. If you ever talk yourself out of it mentally, then you will ultimately be letting your body down, at least when it comes to trying to achieve your physical goals.

Returning to the story, my next mistake was to identify my Russian rival as a big threat. I became aware of others, and began to judge myself by using other people's standards. This, in turn, created doubts in mind, and these doubts escalated. The end result is that I didn't perform as well as I would have liked to have done or, indeed, should have done. The reason is that, long before I was physically beaten into second place, I had mentally defeated myself. Looking back, I was also crazy to change my whole routine in a reaction to the new conditions I found myself experiencing for the first time. At the time it made sense, but if I had prepared myself for the heat I would have undergone my preparations and would have walked into the stadium in a better frame of mind, as opposed to starting the competition doubting my preparation.

The big crowd also hit me when, again, I should have been prepared for it. I should have visualized it enough times beforehand so that when the event became a reality I was already used to it. The number of people had the right effect on me in motivational terms, but not on my ability to focus, which meant that yet more self-doubt appeared. This self-doubt became all-consuming when I saw that my favourite javelin was not going to be used, and then, when the measuring device failed, I turned myself into a mental wreck.

In summing up the story, then, my defeat can boil down to one simple fact: my preparation was appalling. I was the hot favourite to win the World Junior Championships Gold Medal, but, in the end, due to my preparations, I did well even to claim second place.

Of course, everyone has self-doubt. There is nobody in the world who does not suffer from this, no matter how confident they may appear. Like everyone else, I have great moments of self-doubt, but I have learned, on the whole, to mask and control it.

A particularly good method of doing this is suggested by one of my favourite writers in understanding the process of human behaviour, W. Timothy Gallwey. He used a golfing scenario to put across his antidote to self-doubt. When you are putting it is easy to doubt whether the ball will end up in the hole. As Gallwey walked out onto the first putting green, he spoke out aloud: 'I am a good putter, I putt well. I am a good putter, I putt well.' He said this to himself over and over again, and then proceeded to sink his putts. What he is really saying is that we can become what we think. Therefore, what we think has to be the desired effect of what we are going to become.

It goes back to role-playing. Remember, when I am sprinting down the throwers' run-up, I want to feel like a cheetah, but when I unleash the javelin, I want to feel like it is a clap of thunder. By saying, and therefore convincing yourself, that you are a good putter, you can become one. Similarly, if you have to deliver a speech at a convention, telling yourself, over and again, that you are a brilliant speaker, will improve your performance because you've balanced your self-doubt with positive imagery.

In conclusion, our preparation is predominantly in our control. It is everyone's job, whether in sport or business, to make it as likely as possible that we are going to succeed. And to achieve this, we must be prepared for the unexpected, so that we can respond in a positive manner. This is a part of our mental make-up that can be trained, just as our bodies can be.

The way our emotions react to our imagery and role-playing will obviously have a direct effect on our excitement, which also plays an important part in our ability to perform. It is the excitement, or arousal, level that will ultimately control our ability to react in any given situation.

5. AROUSAL

··

While disciplines such as motivation, goal-setting and visualization can be consciously introduced by you, excitement, or arousal, is a natural emotion that can either work for or against you. It is obviously important to be aroused by something, whether in sport or in life, that you are about to experience. A lack of excitement is sure to produce a lacklustre performance, but an overdose of arousal can also lead to disappointing results. While the process of arousal may be natural, you can still learn how to control this important emotion in order to improve your chances of success.

STORY ··

You must be able to recognize when you need to become more excited or, alternatively, when you are clearly overaroused. In the following example, I began to get it wrong, but managed to salvage the situation from what was looking like a potential disaster.

As a child, I was always dreaming about competing in the Olympic Games. At first I wanted to be like Steve Ovett or Sebastian Coe, but by the time I was 14 my heart and mind were set on throwing the javelin as far as I possibly could. Right from the age of seven, during the 1976 Montreal Olympics, I remember my father becoming extremely excited about the athletics events taking place. By the time the Moscow Olympics took place in 1980 I, too, was hooked.

When I started competing in the javelin as a teenager, I used to pretend that I was throwing in the Olympic final. It seemed to give me an edge, an increase in concentration and attention needed to produce the desired performance. I would pretend that I was standing on the runway next to the great javelin throwers of the time. I never understood why, but this made the art of competitive javelin throwing much more fun.

As you have read earlier in this book, I came fourth in the 1988 Olympic trials, and therefore just missed out on a place in the British team. Instead, I watched the javelin competition avidly on television, round by round, almost mimicking the kind of feelings and emotions that I thought each athlete might be going through.

By the time I arrived at the Barcelona Olympics, four years later, I thought I was ready. Those particular Games seemed to have everything: history, glamour, virtually every country in the world participating, and all in a wonderful setting. I had watched some of the Games on television before I flew out to Spain, and so I knew what to expect.

However, the emotions I expected were doubled when I actually arrived. Just mention the word 'Olympics' to me, and I feel a great deal of excitement, conjured up from nowhere. Forget about the World Championships, even if the huge crowds and the opposition are the same. There is something extra special about the Olympics for me.

When I first walked into the stadium to compete, and caught sight of the crowd, and felt the atmosphere, I filled up with fear. The excitement became exaggerated beyond belief. I was unable to control my mind's thoughts and so, without focus, I was aware of too many things around me – like the size of the crowd and the announcer's voice over the stadium's tannoy system.

In short, I was extremely excited, but to a point where I was wondering what was going to happen next. Even though I had competed in major championships before, I suddenly found myself in a confused state, unclear about both the competition's procedure, and my own, carefully thought out mental preparation.

A good 15 minutes passed before I was able to settle myself

down and realize that I did have some mental skills that could help me to deal with the situation. I began to focus and block out what was around me, particularly remembering a good training session I had carried out recently. In other words, I relived the past in order to get a feeling of confidence. Within five minutes I was in a far better and more relaxed frame of mind. The fear had gone, I had returned to the present again, and I was suddenly enjoying the experience and looking forward to the final. All this had been achieved by consciously following the mental techniques I had begun to use.

Then the announcer introduced me as the current world record holder. This confused me because my great rival, Jan Zelezny, had beaten my mark earlier that summer. It was only later that I was to discover that the javelin he used was deemed to be illegal, and that the International Amateur Athletics Federation (IAAF) had therefore reinstated me as the world record holder. Even though I did not know this at the time, hearing my name in this light again provided a real boost. It reminded me how good I can be.

Early on in the final, however, Zelezny produced an 89-metre-plus throw, which proved to be good enough to win the Olympic Gold Medal. In contrast, my first few rounds did not produce anything like I had planned. My motivation could not be questioned, nor could large elements of my mental preparation. Even physically, although by no means perfect, I felt I was in adequate enough condition to mount a real challenge for the Olympic title.

The problem was, I was trying too hard. I could feel the tension in my muscles because I was so excited. I was anxious about what was going to happen, and therefore, because I was not living in real time, everything seemed to happen quickly, indeed too quickly for me to control.

I did not understand at the time that I should have calmed myself down, and used relaxation techniques to bring down the level of excitement. But this was the Olympics, and the whole experience, first time round, proved a little too much.

At least I had enough experience of sports psychology by then to recognize the problem after the third round of the final. I relaxed, to the point of feeling as if I were back in control of all my mental and physical faculties, while aware of – but not distracted by – everything taking place around me.

The fact is, however, that I then suffered a physical breakdown in the fourth round, tearing my adductor muscle, which effectively removed me from the running. At least I came away with a Bronze Medal, achieved through my fourth- round, injury-making effort, but I had come to Barcelona intending to win the Gold Medal.

Looking back, I attribute this relative 'failure' first to being overaroused, and second, to my fourth-round injury. It was my first experience of the Olympics, at least in a live sense; to be 22 and competing in such a monumental event is a *huge* mental challenge. I made an attempt to control my excitement, and feel that I nearly pulled it off.

The Barcelona experience can only put me in good stead for the 1996 Atlanta Olympics. I am not expecting the experiences to be exactly the same, but at least I now have a much deeper understanding of the type of emotional effect the Olympics can have on you.

It would be easy to push examples of relative failure to one side but, as I hope you have gathered by now, it is crucial to remember your mistakes, learn why they happened, and then do something about them.

THEORY ....

The level of arousal is determined by the task in hand and the amount of importance we place on it. The trick is first to recognize, and then to respond. The level of arousal can be thought of as a continuum. At one end is a deep sleep, while at the opposite end, the overexcited end, the level of adrenaline pumping is so high that you are filled, initially, with excitement, but then, if it gets too much, by fear. If you were to walk along this continuum 'tunnel', you would become more excited as you drew closer to the fear end, and more bored as you walked towards the deep sleep end. To simplify this, the best place to

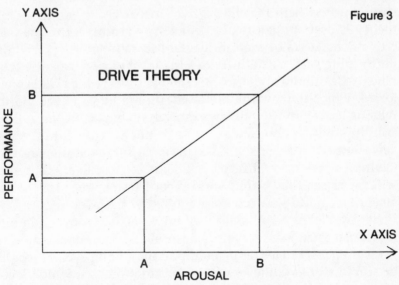

At position A – a low arousal = a low performance
At position B – a higher arousal = a higher performance

find yourself in order to help perform to your optimum level is somewhere between the middle part and the excitement part of the continuum, where you have enough to produce an effective performance, but not too much to hamper yourself.

Over recent years, I have implemented basic psychological principles to decrease or increase levels of arousal. These have been an integral part of my preparation and have proved to be an important element in my overall mental training because, without such knowledge, the effects of arousal, whether positive or negative, can be extremely damaging.

In the graph (*figure 3*), the increase of performance is seen on the *y* axis, while the level of arousal is on the *x* axis. As you can see, while the level of arousal rises, so too does the level of performance, until it reaches the point of optimum arousal. Then it starts to fall away again.

A weightlifter, for instance, performs a gross skill and therefore needs a much higher level of arousal to pump him full of the kind of adrenaline required to produce a sudden burst of strength. It is here that the 'Drive Theory' is applicable. This theory is best applied to a movement requiring a gross whole movement. It states that an increase in nervous energy while performing such a skill increases the level of performance. It is nevertheless more applicable to an event where the skill is well learnt, which is why you are always more likely to see world records broken in front of large crowds on big occasions, rather than in a minor, domestic meeting. While it is usual to see the 100 metres world record be broken, for example, at the Olympics or World Championships, it is most likely that you will never see the javelin world record beaten because a high level of technical skill is required to throw the javelin.

As you learn your skill and improve, so your optimum performance and your levels of arousal can rise. For example, if I was preparing to tee off in an important golfing event, I would be scared stiff, and the fear factor brought on by my high level of arousal could only damage my chances of a good round. In the javelin, however, my well-learned skills mean that I am less likely to break down when I am at a high level of arousal.

This is the case for any movement that requires complex skills. The more complex the skill, the earlier the point of diminishing returns at the same level of arousal. To put it another way, you need to be less aroused to perform to your optimum if you are facing a complex task. You don't want to be too excited because you need to be more focused. If you are a bomb-disposal expert, for example, the last thing you want is a high level of arousal. You don't want to be confronting high explosives in an excited and anxious state. I would be very surprised if these people do not first have to go through some kind of relaxation technique before they go to work. They need to slow themselves down, not quite to the point of boredom and fatigue, but to a point well past excitement, where they are in complete control of their emotions. However, if you are a weightlifter performing a gross skill, you need a much higher level of arousal to pump you full of the kind of adrenaline required to produce a sudden burst of strength.

In the example of the bomb-disposal expert, we are adopting

what is commonly known in sports psychology as the 'optimum arousal theory'. Every individual is different, and this means that we would all respond differently to an increase in arousal, but what is important is that you understand how you can respond and that only you can control and change your emotions. Only you know where your working range is, and only you can know when you are beyond it.

Jonathan Edwards, the world champion, record-holding triple jumper is a classic example. When he emerged from breaking not one, but two world records, on his way to winning the 1995 World Championships Gold Medal in Gothenburg, he later explained, when asked by the media to talk them through the world record jumps, that all he was thinking about was jumping into the sandpit. He became oblivious of the fact that he was competing in the World Championships, in front of a huge, live audience, and a television audience of a billion people. Any excitement he experienced, he slowed down to the extent that he was in total control of his arousal.

As an intermediate golfer, I could apply the optimal arousal theory to my ability to swing a club. Some days, if there is no incentive to try to succeed, my focus will not be acute. Other days, I may want it too much, and then the swing is equally impaired. I remember playing golf with my British rival, Mick Hill, in New Zealand. We were enjoying some warm-weather training in winter, and had already played a number of rounds of golf, when we decided to make the games more interesting.

We started to play for a couple of pounds but, after a while, even that novelty wore off. Mick then made the suggestion that we should buy a particularly tasteless bracelet from the local market. The idea was that the loser would have to wear it until the next time we played.

The result was an obvious increase in motivation and natural arousal although, in this instance instead of wanting to win, the desire was to not lose. It had the desired effect. We produced the best round of golf throughout the trip. We both upped our game enormously. With one hole remaining, I was down one and I needed to dig deep to claw back the deficit. My heart was pumping and my attention was less focused as a result of becoming too anxious about the prospect of wearing the bracelet.

Ten minutes later, I had to put it on and keep it on for the next three days until our next game of golf. I had gone past my optimum level and I was inexperienced both in the skill and in the ability to respond mentally. I have been faced with a very similar situation in the javelin, in which I have been asked to come back from behind.

The realization of impending doom in the javelin can mean an increase in arousal, but because there is a physical and mental skill factor in my event, the normal result is that I throw further. A couple of sports psychologists in the 1970s, Martens and Landers, tested this hypothesis by using a tracing skill that measured arm steadiness. It was designed to measure the effect arousal could have on you. The best results were attained from the people performing under moderate stress – far better results in fact than those recorded by the people exposed to either low or high levels of stress.

One of the most nail-biting finales in sport took place in 1985 when Dennis Taylor defeated Steve Davis 18–17, after finally potting a relatively easy black ball in the very last frame. After two days of playing, in front of a live crowd and a television audience that grew to 18 million viewers, it boiled down to one ball. The tension was clearly enormous for both players, because they each proceeded to miss two attempts at potting the black, which, in practice, they could have done with their eyes shut. The tension and the nerves they both experienced were purely down to negative arousal. They were clearly overaroused, and this led to a detrimental effect. I don't suppose Taylor minds too much now, but it could have cost him the title, as it did for Davis.

While inexperienced performers find themselves thinking about the end when it draws near, efficient performers have been known to be unaware that the end has come. A good example of this is Bobby Charlton when the whistle blew to end the 1966 World Cup final. Even though England had won 4–2, and there had clearly been a lot of goals scored, he was unaware of the final score, and actually had to be told. His job was to tackle, and he was so focused on this element of the game and his own performance, that the outcome was never an issue. As a result, the outcome proved to be the correct one for Charlton. So, arousal is the most significant factor relating to breakdown when we relate psychology to performance. But how do we combat anxious situations?

The first point is an obvious but, nevertheless, important one. Identify what situations make you anxious. This sounds obvious, I know, but it does not matter what anyone else thinks, it is entirely up to you to identify them and write them down. Generally, we know that anxiety develops as a result of a fear of the unknown. Yet, if you can segment the event that is making you anxious, and actually detail what it means to you, and how it affects you before, during and after performing, you could find that the prospect is suddenly not as frightening.

For example, many people become very nervous at the thought of meeting someone very famous, like a member of the royal family. But what is it that makes them nervous? If you see yourself walking up to that person and saying 'Hello', does that thought make you nervous? It usually doesn't. Okay then, does asking the question, 'How are you today?' make you nervous? Again, not really. No, it is the whole picture that is raising your arousal. If you go through the event step by step, your anxiety may be reduced or at least diminished to the point where you regain a greater willingness to proceed.

Another day-to-day example is that of having to make a speech, whether it is at a major business convention, a cricket club dinner, or a best man's speech. No matter who the audience is, most would-be orators will become increasingly anxious as the speech draws nearer. They are not used to standing up and speaking because they are not trained orators.

So, again, what is it about this speech that makes you particularly nervous? Is it standing up out of your chair to start? Is it walking towards your lectern or the audience? Is it getting your papers out and placing them in front of you? Is it reading the first line? Whichever it might be, you need to be fully attentive to the task you are about to perform, and mustn't let your nervous, overaroused state deflect your concentration. Using the deep breathing and centring techniques discussed in the chapter focusing on visualization, calm yourself and your arousal down. Then, introduce part of what you fear and break it down into segments. So, look at yourself standing up to make your speech. Go over it again and again so that, eventually, it no longer seems scary. Try, in particular, to visualize the worst segment, over and over again, until you become more confident with it. Go through this process, segment by segment, until you reach the end of your speech.

The sports psychologists, John Syer and Christopher Connolly, have a skiing analogy to underline this. They knew someone who went on a skiing holiday for the first time and spent a few days on the nursery slopes before being persuaded to be a little bolder. When he stood at the top of the piste and looked down the mountain he began to tell himself that there was no way he was ready for this scary challenge.

The ski instructor, who could see the problem, pointed to a tree fifty yards down the piste and asked if skiing to that point would be too frightening. The novice skier agreed that a short run like that would pose no problems. The instructor then suggested they should both ski to the tree. Suddenly the skier had turned from a frozen state to someone actually skiing on the piste. When they reached the tree, the instructor pointed to the other side of the piste and asked if the skier had a problem skiing over to the next point. Again, they both shot off further down the slope, and continued this process, from point to point, landmark to landmark, until they reached the foot of the mountain.

The next time the skier performed this by himself, missing out alternate points the first time, missing out most of them the second time and then, finally, completing the whole piste without any stoppages. By approaching his task step by step, he immediately reduced the anxiety effect that hinders performance.

How do we know when we are anxious? Sometimes, it is obvious. One minute you are enjoying yourself, the next you have lost sight of your outcome goal, and whatever you are doing has lost its excitement and enjoyment. But other times, you may not immediately recognize this state. Your physical state normally gives the game away. If your muscles suddenly feel tight and tense, then you know immediately that you have a mental problem. You will experience an unwillingness to proceed, which, in turn, will result in slowing down. This will often be associated with an increase in heart rate. Another indication may be the fact that you find it difficult to think clearly, while one of the less obvious, and in many ways most damaging factors, is the change in your perception of time.

I can remember the first time I was asked to be interviewed on television. I was filled with fear at the prospect of what was going to happen. What I couldn't understand was that, both five minutes before and five minutes after the interview, it was a really exciting idea, but the experience of the actual ten-minute interview was anything but exciting. You never have much time to get something right as it happens. Whether it is a sporting event or a speech, it never lasts long. You will always spend much more time preparing for it – and then holding a post-mortem – than you will ever spend actually doing it. That is why it is so important to be living in the present tense. By doing this you prepare yourself for the present, which is obviously vital during your performance.

In general, I have to worry more about being overaroused, but there have been times when a low level of arousal has also threatened my performance. If you return to the continuum example, it is the sleepy, drowsy end of the tunnel you find yourself in when you require more arousal. This often occurs just after a period of overarousal. It is only natural to suffer from a slump after just experiencing a peak, but it is your job to raise yourself enough to continue to perform to your optimum level.

One way to tackle this problem is actually to visualize the impending doom that awaits you. Don't visualize bad habits or techniques, just the actual outcome if you fail to lift yourself. The golfing bracelet story I mentioned earlier highlights this. Cassius Clay, before he changed his name to Muhammed Ali, stated before fighting Henry Cooper that if the British Heavyweight managed to knock him down, he would not

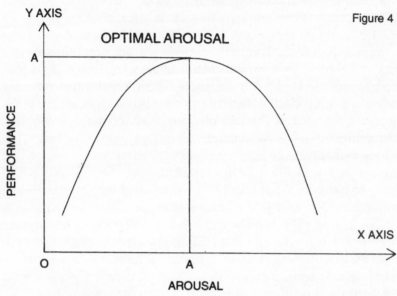

Point A = optimum
Any higher or lower arousal would mean a reduced performance

return to America for three months. By doing this, he increased his desire not to lose.

Of course, you could turn it around the other way, and imagine the reward. This process should only be used when trying to up your arousal. As I have said in the goal-setting chapter, once you have recognized your outcome goal, you should then concentrate first on your process and then on your performance goals. But there are occasions in sports psychology when you need to break the rules, and here is one of them. By thinking of your outcome goal, and its subsequent rewards, this should arouse you out of your drowsy, disinterested state, but as soon as you have achieved this, get back to the present, and to the performance and then, ultimately, the process goal.

By having an understanding of what makes you, as an individual, anxious or relaxed, you can manipulate your level of arousal. By doing this, you will have a tool capable of bringing your arousal level into the optimum area, thus maximizing your performance as outlined in the optimal arousal theory diagram (*figure 4*).

Your mind rarely knows the difference between imagery and reality. This is an extremely important point. You can, effectively, pull the wool over your your mind's eyes by convincing it that what in fact is imagery can also be taken for reality. This underlines the need to visualize. If we can imagine something to the point where it seems to have happened, the effect is the same, and the result is an increase in arousal.

SUMMARY ....

Your level of arousal and the intensity of your motivation are inextricably linked. By increasing the level of one of these components, it can have a direct effect on increasing the level of the other. This should therefore be viewed as a useful tool in the process of manipulating your own psyche.

In the story about the Olympics, my level of arousal was almost inevitable. I had thought about the Olympics from an early age, and this had been continually reinforced throughout my life. If you consider the time span involved, my expectations about competing in Barcelona were huge. I had spent the best part of 15 years getting excited about what would probably take 90 minutes.

Missing out on the 1988 Seoul Olympics only added to this excitement, because it meant I was out to make amends. A massive amount of excitement and anxiety naturally stemmed from all of this. I think the level of arousal I experienced on that day was the highest I have ever felt. If I had seen a ghost, I do not believe I could have been more aroused.

This is not necessarily a bad thing for an athlete. But it was my job to make sure that my response to this incredibly high arousal was correct. I would dearly hope that I experience a similar high arousal when I compete in the 1996 Olympics in Atlanta. This time, however, I will know how to react.

If you want something badly enough, then you should be able

to concentrate on the job in hand, and not on what is making you so anxious. It is your concentration on your anxiety that makes you more anxious. This can be translated as fear of making a mistake. Well, the mistake is not the initial one, but the failure to respond to the mistake. Successful people will always learn from their mistakes, and will not let the negative arousal that stems from these mistakes obstruct their path.

I now know that my fears experienced during the Barcelona Olympics would not have happened if I had turned the unknown into the known by using step-by-step visualization to transform them into the familiar. It is very hard for any sportsperson to admit this, but looking back at Barcelona, even though I still achieved a Bronze Medal, I can now say that I began to choke. I was out of touch with my body, everything became rushed and I was unable to respond to being overaroused. Because I had a limited understanding of the mind by then, I was able to turn it round by the fourth round, which, I think, speaks volumes for the powers of the mind. Most people have experienced the contrasting feelings of choking and of being in what I have termed 'the zone'.

My summer of 1994 highlights both the damaging experiences of high and low arousal. The European Championships were the highlight of that season, especially for me. I had experienced three disappointing years, and desperately needed a good result. Sure enough, I experienced an optimum in my arousal, but I was able to deal with it by breaking down the process of events into tactical and process goals, and by visualization. I applied the mental brakes to my excitements and fears and found myself back in 'the zone'.

Not surprisingly, and especially after I had won the Gold Medal, I then experienced a slump after the European Championships ended. This could have been an immense problem because, just one week later, I found myself in Victoria, Canada, defending my Commonwealth title. I was in a mental trough. My arousal was at rock bottom, I felt unmotivated, tired and sluggish.

I can particularly remember walking from the warm-up area to the track as if walking to a run-of-the-mill training session.

Obviously, I was not overexcited at the prospect of competing. If I compare this to a fortnight earlier, when I was in a very nervous state of mind, the contrast is extremely clear. Even when I got to the track, placed my bag down, put my spikes on, and picked up my javelin, a point at which I would normally expect an increase in arousal, I was still in a very noncommittal mood. I was aware of the crowd, other throwers' movements, and other external factors, which I should have been – and normally am – oblivious of.

I was able to lift myself up sufficiently to win the Commonwealth Gold Medal by repeatedly telling myself that this was the Commonwealth Games, a major championship, with millions of people watching live and on television. I reminded myself that it was my title, my Gold Medal, and that I was expected to win. There was a Gold Medal waiting with my name on it, but if I did not get my backside into gear it would be taken away from me.

I actually visualized this happening, using the desire not to lose process to help me awake from my mental sleep. All this clearly worked because the level of arousal was raised enough for me to enter 'the zone' and snuff out everything else happening around me.

I remember, prior to the actual European final, being fearful, anxious and excited in the athletes' check-in room. I was able to control these feelings, however, and keep right on the borderline between positive and negative arousal, but in the Commonwealth Games check-in room I was chatting away to everyone with my blinkers off. I even began the final in this state of mind. Fortunately, I realized my predicament in time, which is when I reminded myself of what was at stake. I also imagined that Mick Hill, who ended up second behind me, had actually thrown 85 metres, which, on the day, would have beaten my best throw. I imagined myself lying in third place and, again, used the desire-not-to-lose approach to pull me through.

What was especially satisfying about that summer, apart from the obvious results, was that I was able to achieve my outcome goals, even though I experienced totally contrasting levels of arousal. Physically, there was absolutely no difference between the 'me' at the European Championships and the 'me' at the Commonwealth Games, but there was clearly a huge mental difference. If I had not applied my mind correctly, I might have ended up with nothing that summer, or become European champion one week, and a complete failure the next week in Canada.

Clearly, both in visualization and arousal, the ability to use relaxation techniques, including centring, is vitally important. The crux of relaxation is not only being able to decrease arousal, but also being able to visualize fully.

6. CONCENTRATION AND RELAXATION

··

You cannot apply yourself to any of the psychological disciplines already outlined in this book unless you are concentrating. It is inevitable that your concentration and level of relaxation are inextricably linked.

I have touched on relaxation in this book, especially in the chapter devoted to visualization, but it is now time to look, more deeply, at both concentration and relaxation in psychological terms.

STORY ···

As you can see from the previous chapter, I have been known to get it right as well. In this story, the ability, not only to concentrate and relax, but also to link the two together, pays enormous dividends.

My first year in senior, international athletics, had been extremely successful for me. 1989 proved to be the year when I won the overall Grand Prix title, and was also rated as the world's number one. But the following year, 1990, posed a whole new set of goals for me, which would test my physical strength and my ability to handle serious pressure.

This seemed to be heightened by an expectation, not only from my family, friends and the media, but also from myself. It was a task, however, that I relished. The first test came early in the year in Auckland, at the Commonwealth Games. The physical preparation for the Games took place in Los Angeles.

The training went well, and I was throwing distances that I felt would be enough to win the Gold Medal. In short, I had no doubts that I would win.

Ten days before the start of the Games I made my way from the States to New Zealand, to finalize my preparations, while my coach, John Trower, returned home to England. All of a sudden, I lost my concentration.

I was already beginning to doubt myself when Gavin Lovegrove, one of my chief rivals for the Gold Medal, did something to exacerbate my feelings. Lovegrove, a Kiwi who would be throwing in front of a home crowd, turned up a couple of days before the start of the Games while Mick Hill and I were training. He suddenly appeared from nowhere, in a very blessed and confident manner, and within 10 minutes produced an 85-metre throw, before packing his bags and leaving again.

It was a statement, and it had the desired effect on me. All I could see was Lovegrove reproducing this kind of form during the actual final, while I was struggling to better the 80-metre mark. Immediately, the distances I was achieving in training reduced.

The problem was obvious because of these distances, but the reasons were not. I tried to blame jet lag for my sudden loss of form in training, but the end result was that John Trower had to jump back on a plane and come down to New Zealand for a couple of days.

He arrived the day before the start of the javelin competition and, after one long training session, I was able to focus again on the task in hand. Suddenly, instead of questioning myself, and feeling anxious about the Games, I found myself back in the present tense. The training session began with a jog together, something that I was familiar with. During this run, I was able to bounce some thoughts and ideas off John, which immediately had the desired effect of reconfirming that all my preparation was in place. We then went through a typical training session, excluding the actual throws and replacing them with some run-ups, to reinforce the rhythms and positions that had been missing in the preceding few days in my mind. Simply by having John present at this session was enough to give me the necessary push to focus effectively.

Although John did make a couple of technical suggestions, his most important contribution was to make me feel confident again, by telling me how good I looked, in my technique, my preparation and my general shape. This gave me the confidence to relax, which was the first time it dawned on me how powerful an asset a totally relaxed state of mind can be.

The next day I began my warm-up in a good frame of mind, and although one or two inevitable problems arose, such as my training shoe falling apart, they did not manifest themselves as mental doubts, which would have impaired my performance. Instead, they were dealt with and forgotten, thus enabling me to perform well. My first-round effort was a throw of 84.90 metres. On the day, this was more than enough to see off the opposition. The next goal was to tackle the world record, which I was within a couple of metres of breaking. The closest I came to this mark came in the sixth and last round, when I recorded a throw of 86.02 metres, which was not enough to set a new world best, but good enough to break my own British and Commonwealth record. This gave me a very positive start to what was going to prove to be an extremely successful season.

Because the Commonwealth Games were in February 1990, I felt that breaking the world record was a realistic goal that would be a part of my preparation for the European Championships in Split, later in the summer. The fact that a Swede called Patrick Boden later increased the record to 89.10 metres did not deflate my confidence. I broke my own best at a Cardiff meeting in May, with a throw of 88.54 metres, and I knew that I had the ability to produce the world's best.

The day to break the world record came at the Stockholm meeting, where, in opposition, I faced Boden on his home turf. As I warmed up on a particularly still and balmy evening, I felt particularly focused. The warm-up was carried out in a very relaxed manner – in fact, I was almost too relaxed. As I entered the stadium I didn't really feel ready to throw. It was a subsequent sense of urgency that provided a sudden rush of adrenaline, making me feel excited and almost fearful of the events that I felt were about to happen. My warm-up throws were well under par, which caused a second surge of adrenaline. At no point during the warm-up did I think that I was about to break the world record. My focus was directed towards winning and, more importantly, the process goals that would enable me to do just that. I remember being totally focused as I ran down the runway before delivering the javelin. In performing this act, everything felt absolutely right. I was relaxed, but also aroused by a slight fear of what I knew well could happen that night. I was, if you like, the actor moments before the curtain rises. He's nervous, and his stomach is churning, but he also knows that he has learned his lines properly, which gives him an inner confidence.

Subsequently, in my very first throw, I produced 89.58 metres, for a new world record by 40 centimetres. My immediate reaction was to take my boots off. I knew that my work was done for the night, and I knew that Boden would not be up for a fight after seeing me break his mark.

A week later in Oslo, I came up against Jan Zelezny, the man who had already become my main rival in world athletics. He broke my world record in the fourth round with 89.66. This was only 8 centimetres further, so I obviously felt that this new mark was well within my reach, but I failed to come up with a good enough answer. In hindsight, I failed in Oslo because I was just not relaxed enough. I had not been beaten all summer, and my reaction to Zelezny's throw was to become too tense.

Still, I did not have to wait long for another chance. A week later, at Crystal Palace, I broke the world record for the second time that summer, in front of my home crowd. Zelezny had been trying too hard for a big throw in the early rounds, while I was leading the competition with a throw of 86 metres. In the third round, I produced a throw of 89 metres, which meant by the time I stood on the runway for my fourth-round effort, I knew the record was on. The atmosphere that night was electric, yet despite all the noise and pressure, I was really able to concentrate on my final preparations before actually throwing. If ever I knew I was going to break the world record it was then. I've mentioned it a number of times already in this book, but once again I found myself completely in 'the mental zone'. The actual measurement – 90.98 metres – absolutely smashed Zelezny out of sight, at least on that night. Predictably, he was to bounce back later.

A fortnight after the Crystal Palace meeting, I flew out to Split for the European Championships. This was the biggest task I had ever faced because, although I had proved I could throw the javelin a long way, and although I had won the Commonwealth Gold Medal earlier in the year, this was by far the most important championship I was to compete in at that point of my career, where my mental strength would be severely tested.

During the first round of the final it began to rain. It turned into a downpour, with the rain was bouncing off the track. The officials wanted to delay the competition a couple of throws before it was my first turn. By the time I stepped up to begin my account, they were insisting that they had to stop the competition.

I was determined to get a throw out. At this stage, the lead was only 82 metres and I didn't fancy sitting in a small room for ages until the rain stopped without having recorded at least one throw. I also had a picture in my mind of what I was going to produce, which gave me a great feeling of confidence.

I walked back to the start of the runway and stood, expectantly, in the rain, making it clear that I intended to throw. I then made my mind drift back to the kind of feelings I had just prior to my 90 metres world record, before consciously returning to the present tense. The level of concentration was enormous, and resulted in a throw of 85 metres. This may not seem huge compared to my world record, but remember that records in the javelin are not often broken in the major championships.

We were all then rushed off to a shelter, where we had to wait 40 minutes, just long enough for everyone else to think how far 85 metres seemed in the rain. I remember making a conscious effort to try and relax. I had five rounds to go, and I did not want the fact that I was leading the European Championships to affect my mental state. Although I had much to learn about psychology, I knew enough to try and visualize the rest of the competition, which put me in good stead for when the rain finally stopped. The next four rounds passed by with no change, and no threat to my leading throw. By the time I stepped up in the last round, I knew I had already won. All the people who could have threatened me had completed their six throws.

I remember feeling completely relaxed at this stage. I knew I had won, but I still convinced myself that someone else was leading in order to motivate myself. I therefore possessed the near perfect combination for a peak performance: total concentration, because I had to beat this imaginary leading throw, mixed with a high level of relaxation, which, in turn, produced supreme confidence. The result was 87.66 metres, a throw that rubbed salt deeper into the opposition's wounds, and, in my book, was one of my best ever major championship throws.

As a result of all my success that year, I was then asked to do the television and radio rounds. It was a great experience appearing on shows like *A Question of Sport* but the programme that particularly comes to mind is *Wogan*, which, back in 1990, was the most popular chat show on British television.

This was new territory for me. I was asked on because of my skills as a javelin thrower, not because I was skilled as a public speaker. I remember clearly the sequence of events that took place, and relate it to a javelin competition.

I had to wait in what TV refers to as the 'Green Room', where all guests are wined and dined before they make their on-screen appearance. My mind was jumping ahead and I was anxious about what was going to happen when I walked on, in front of a live audience. I was then led to the side of the set, where I stood in the wings waiting for my cue to walk onto the stage.

I felt as nervous then as I have ever done in any javelin competition. I then decided to put it all into perspective, reminding myself that I had competed in front of millions in the sports arena. I then asked myself what I would be doing if I was about to start a competition. The answer was not just to stand there and admit to myself how nervous I felt, but to go through a sequence of mental events. This is precisely what I did then before walking on to be interviewed by Sue Lawley, who was standing in for Terry Wogan that night.

I remember performing a little visualization session, and also some relaxation techniques. Instead of being frightened by the whole concept, I fragmented the interview, so that the thought of walking on set, sitting down, and then answering a few questions about myself no longer made me feel anxious. By breaking it all down, I suddenly felt remarkably relaxed. I concentrated on these immediate skills, rather than on the fact that there would be cameras, a live audience and a six-million TV audience.

When I compete in a stadium, there are always a lot of TV cameras milling around the warm-up area, the runway and the actual field. My concentration is normally so great that I never notice them then, so why should I have noticed them on the *Wogan* set?

This was probably the first time that I understood that the mental skills I practised as a javelin thrower could actually spill over into everyday life, making me able to handle such situations. While I was actually answering Sue Lawley's questions, I made a big point of concentrating on what I was saying. By doing this, I was able to ignore both the on-set distractions, and the noise from the crowd, who had just been whooped up into a frenzy by Alan Alda, who had been the previous guest. I may have been desperately nervous beforehand, but thanks to psychological techniques learned on the sports field, I was able to perform well in – what was for me – an entirely new environment. It rounded off a memorable summer.

THEORY

Relaxation can be viewed as a conscious ability to turn your attention away from possible distractions and focus on the important skills required to fulfil your process goals. I emphasize the word 'conscious' because the ability to relax mentally is very much a skill, just like any other part of the physical or mental preparation. Because it is a skill, it is something we can learn to do.

The correct balance between increased relaxation and concentration should be one of our major goals. Relaxation and concentration are inextricably linked. Try and visualize a day, or an event, in which you have performed optimally. Try and remember how everything just seemed to come together, almost without effort. How did everything feel before, during and after that particular moment? For me, it was probably that night at Crystal Palace, when I recaptured the world javelin record.

When you have a clear picture in your own mind, note down the feelings induced by reliving the moment. Then compare them to normal, everyday feelings. There should be a difference, which should be noted and remembered. If you can recapture the feelings and emotions experienced when you performed to your optimal level, you should be able to get close to repeating your performance.

Concentration is obviously synonymous with our ability to perform. Some people are able to control this on a daily basis, because concentration is nothing more than blocking out the unwanted. It can be improved if practised, and there are different factors that will enable us to do this more effectively.

You must be disciplined enough to work in the present tense. The mind is able to slow down and, ultimately, to concentrate. Research shows that, by relaxing, we can allow the left and right sides of our brain to work together and communicate with each other. The left-hand side of the brain is the far more mathematical, logical and analytical side, and can be very effective when it comes to analysing and assessing our performance it can also be very destructive by obstructing the flow of thoughts in the right-hand side. By performing some simple relaxation techniques we can limit the level of distraction and increase our ability to concentrate.

As I outlined in the previous chapter, the relaxation of the mind and the arousal you may well be experiencing, will help you perform in a stressful situation. Focusing on general movements is the next key. In other words, concentrate on everyday, whole movements rather than minor, technical movements, for example, walking or sitting in a chair. It is easier to stay relaxed while performing these simple, everyday tasks, and by concentrating on a key aspect of them, we will increase our focus internally, and therefore shift away from potential distractions.

Secondly, interest has to play an important part in concentration. Obviously, if we are more interested in a given task, the more likely we are to concentrate – reading a newspaper article that particularly catches the eye, for instance. However, you can actually turn this around. By concentrating more on something, you will inevitably be more interested. You can look at anything and quickly pass over it, but if you look closer, and with a greater attention to detail, you will automatically become more interested in it.

Take driving a car, which is technically a complex procedure. Changing gears, applying your feet to three different pedals and manoeuvring the car demands a great deal of concentration. By making all the individual movements autonomous without eradicating the overall awareness required for driving, you will notice the increased smoothness of your performance.

Or, take slouching in a chair. If you discipline yourself to sit up straight each time you do this, sooner or later it will become second nature to you. This is exactly how you learn to drive. You concentrate on an aspect, like changing gears, until you have mastered it sufficiently to keep on performing this task while incorporating others and, effectively, splitting the mind. What you are actually doing is still concentrating on the aspect of driving you are required to perform while scanning and processing everything else going on around you at the same time.

In a sporting context, I remember being told by another novice golfer how he focused on one particular part of the ball's dimple. By concentrating hard on this, it made him more interested in the ball and the club head. He forgot about all the external distractions, like the rain, and concentrated on the specific job in hand.

The ultimate is to be in a state in which you are relaxed *and* concentrating, especially on your breathing. As discussed in the previous chapter, the centering part of relaxation is an important first step towards a visualization process. It decreases our level of arousal, which gives us a better chance of finding the 'zone'.

To expand further from centering, and to achieve an ever deeper level of relaxation, I often use a technique called 'Modal

10' *(figure 5)*, which was developed by Brian Miller, a sports psychologist.

The process begins by using the centering method that was used in the chapter on visualization, whereby you sit in a comfortable and symmetrical position, shut your eyes and concentrate on your breathing. Then, divide your body up into segments, which you should pay particular attention to, as you move around your body. Always begin with the stomach, which is your centre of gravity and the place where all movement is initiated. Then go up to the chest, the lower back, the right leg, the upper thigh, the left leg and thigh, both arms and then up to the top of the back, moving around the body in a way that breaks up the body allowing you to focus on particular segments.

A similar method is to use the clock technique *(figure 5)*, which divides the body up into 12 sections in a clockwise direction. You then move around the body in the same way that a hand moves around a clock face, systematically relaxing each muscle as you come to it. Once you have done this, you move on to the next but, like the driver in the car, you are still scanning and, therefore, relaxing the muscles you have already visited. So, the clock technique begins with the left arm, and moves down to the left forearm, before proceeding to the chest, down to the stomach, the left thigh, the leg, the right leg, then the right thigh, before moving up the right arm, then your neck, and finishes with your head.

The 'Modal 10' technique should take about 12 minutes to complete, while the clock method should take a little longer. These methods are more effective in the longer term, enabling you to relax in preparation for competition, or in a post-competitive state. During the actual event, however, these techniques would not be so appropriate.

Instead, you should be looking at something along the lines of centring, combining it with your ability to pick out and concentrate on details relevant to the task ahead. Centering can be learnt very quickly if you apply your mind to it and concentrate. This combination will result in a state of deep concentration, but still in a relaxed manner.

CLOCK RELAXATION   MODAL TEN RELAXATION

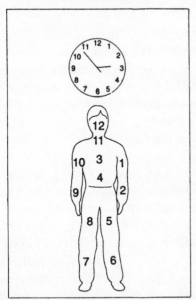 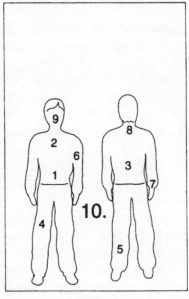

Figure 5

It all boils down to training your mind. If you implement these techniques when you face moments of high stress, you should be able to reduce the tension sufficiently to turn the fear factor to your advantage.

So, the process you have to remember is:

• Slow down heart rate and breathing, and internalize your thoughts by blocking out external distractions.
• Focus on a gross or simple skill, like walking or sitting listening to music. I find that when I am warming up I like to listen to music and jog at the same time. By doing this, the music deflects everything else around me, allowing me to concentrate on my jogging, which then becomes increasingly more comfortable.
• By retaining the relaxation and the concentration, the bigger

skill warrants only a subliminal focus, allowing you to give greater detail to the actual process skills.

Confidence will come as soon as you have practised this enough times to start feeling the benefits of the process, and if you can become consistent, you will breed a confidence that will rarely falter. Of course, the formula is always changing in life, which means that your desires and needs change with it but, as was stated in the goal-setting chapter, if you can keep on reassessing and refocusing you should be able to continue using this formula.

This is where experience always comes in handy. In football, for example, a player will lose his pace as he gets older, but his mental experience should enable him to compensate with better timing. A good example of this is Ruud Gullit. He may be in the twilight of his career, but he is still a wonderfully stylish player who creates more time to allow himself to pass the ball. He knows the state of mind he needs when it comes to competing, and he knows how to obtain it. His process skills are also well determined, and then well learnt.

Of course you can get to the top in anything you do using nothing much more than a naïve confidence. As you have read, I am as good an example as anyone here. But people who achieve this do not stay at the top. I never questioned myself, nor bothered to think about relaxing by concentrating first on external matters, before internalizing them. I just went out and threw the damn thing.

But if I had known how important a part relaxation plays in combating stress and tension, I am sure that some of the mistakes I have made could have been foreseen and avoided, both in sport and in everyday life. Now, having acquired a greater understanding of this subject, I find that it applies to far more areas than I first envisaged. The main point I have taken from this theory is the increase in my ability to focus on the detail of my process goals, which comes about through the simple exercise of living in the present tense, thus increasing my attention to detail.

SUMMARY ....

Everything I have talked about so far in this chapter has been geared towards a mental ability. The psychological aspects of concentration and relaxation are as deep as you can get, certainly in sports psychology, and it would seem as though there is little or no physical connection.

Actually, this is not quite the case. When you relax, you enjoy a decrease of tension in your muscles, and a reduction in your heart beat, two crucial responses that can only improve your performance. In turn, this leads to a decrease in blood pressure and an increase in ability to respond physically. It is now generally accepted that the skill of relaxation can only be beneficial if practised during all phases of the process: long-term preparation, last-minute practice, or even during the event.

If you analyse my story at the beginning of this chapter, you can soon identify the important role that concentration and relaxation play in my success. It amazes me that it is very common for an athlete suddenly to lose confidence on the eve of a major event. Well, we are all human, and it would be impossible to change this. One of the recurring themes of this book rears its head again here. You cannot change what are natural, human emotions, but you can change your response to these emotions if you stay in touch with your process goals, and learn to relax.

When I saw Gavin Lovegrove produce that throw in training, my confidence was reduced as a result of a decrease in my throwing distance, which was brought on by a lack of relaxation, and a lack of concentration on the skills required to achieve my process goals. I remember walking around the athlete's village the day before the start of the Commonwealth Games with my mind focusing on other matters. It should have been on the present tense – being in Auckland because I was going to win a Gold Medal. It is very easy to drift out of the present tense, but if your focus and relaxation become a matter of a conscious decision, you should be in a much better position to respond to a shift in your confidence. While my coach was not with me, I was not living in the present tense and lost this edge.

But when he arrived in New Zealand, he was able to remind me of the present scenario. His verbal pick-me-ups gave me the ability to relax more. I had not changed in any physical way, and if I had been psychologically more experienced, I might not have needed such encouragement, but, back in 1990, it was just the tonic I needed.

Moving on to Oslo, where Jan Zelezny took away my world record, one of the main reasons why I didn't throw further that evening was because I was not relaxed enough. I was extremely focused, but, by failing to relax, I became tense, and, considering the level required to beat Zelezny that night, the odds were stacked too much against me.

It was a different situation altogether at Crystal Palace, where I quickly found myself in the 'zone'. This was my first successful experience of reliving past victories in order to create more success in the present tense. I relaxed and reminded myself of everything I had done in the build-up to the previous 90-metre throw. I knew I only needed to add a little extra and the world record was there for the taking.

It worked to equal effect at the European Championships, where I concentrated so hard on reliving my world record throw that I walked straight past my coach on the way to the athletes' room without seeing him. My mind was therefore split between the memories and feelings of when I was last in the correct mental zone, and the need to remain in the present tense.

As the story also explained, I was then able to put to good use relaxation techniques acquired in the sports stadium when I appeared on *Wogan*. It turned me from a bag of nerves into someone well able to handle the situation.

A proven method of putting the theories into practice is to build up a ritual to increase both our concentration and relaxation, both internally and, as a result of our performance, externally. The trick is to build up a pattern that becomes the norm each time before the start of an event.

When it comes to sport, Linford Christie is a classic example here. His concentration, just before the start of a 100 metres race, is so intense that a bomb could explode next to him without creating any kind of distraction. At a glance he looks arrogant, but a closer inspection reveals that he is totally focused on the race. Whether he is in Zurich, Rome or Brussels, he goes through the same procedure, bending down, shaking his legs, springing up and down on the spot, and so on.

In contrast, one of his main rivals, America's Dennis Mitchell, jumps around the starting blocks, shouting and clapping his hands. His preparation is the exact opposite to Christie's. But they are both merely performing a ritual that they know has, in the past, helped them to produce their optimum performance. Even though Mitchell finds a noisier way of doing it, he is nevertheless using his method to relax and concentrate to good effect.

Another good example would be Bjorn Borg and John McEnroe. They were two great rivals on the tennis court but, mentally, they could not have been more different. While Borg remained ice cool, never allowing his emotions to become external, McEnroe often exposed his red-hot emotions to the public. Yet it was noticeable how McEnroe rarely lost a point after one of his outbursts. This was his way of relaxing and regaining concentration. He performed this ritual each time to help him refocus.

I put my knowledge of relaxation techniques to good use in 1995 when I was invited to Buckingham Palace to collect an MBE from the Queen. For some reason, it was one of the most nerve-wracking experiences of my life. All I had to do was to stand in a room, with around 200 other people all in their top hats, and then walk across the hall, turn, face the Queen, walk two steps forward, answer a question, and then retreat two steps backwards before walking off. In theory, simple!

Yet, the high arousal I felt automatically made my concentration wander. I actually felt it necessary to visualize walking across the hall a few times to ensure that, when the time came, I would not get it wrong. I then went through the centering technique, focusing on the carpet and breathing deeply. The small piece of carpet I concentrated on became the only thing that mattered to me in the room.

As a result, it all went smoothly, except for the part I had not bothered to visualize, which was when I was supposed to walk backwards having received my award. I actually turned round, as if to walk normally, before I remembered and turned round again to walk backwards.

So, in a final summary, the key point is to concentrate fully on an aspect of your task, which will then help you to scan the whole picture. The more you can block out other distractions, the better your chances of being relaxed, and the more relaxed you are, the better the end result. It is asking a lot of a sportsperson, for example, to be totally relaxed before the most important competition of his or her life, in front of an audience of many millions, but, by using a psychological process, and a series of techniques suited to personal needs, it can be done, by repeating a ritual that increases concentration and allows us relaxation.

Now that every area has been examined in the build-up to the actual event, it is high time that I finally looked at the actual day when, hopefully, your outcome goals will be realized.

7. COMPETITION

So this is the day. This is what everything has been geared to. All that preparation, all that effort, and all that time, and now it all boils down to this one moment. If you think that you have done everything psychologically possible in readiness for the day of competition, then that is obviously good. But, it would be a grave mistake if you thought that, at this late stage, the die is cast, and there is nothing you can now do to alter the course of events. Competition itself is an important ingredient in the psychological process.

STORY ....

In the following story, I am going to use a 'Groundhog Day' technique to explain how to, and how not to, achieve your final outcome goals on the big day. In other words, I am going to recreate two, contrasting days in my career: one when I made just about every mistake in the book; another, when I more or less got it dead right. The way not to do it was exemplified at the 1991 World Championships in Tokyo, and if that day had been my 'Groundhog Day', I would have replaced it with the day, three years later, when I won the European Gold Medal.

It is one week before the world championships begin in Tokyo in 1991. I have already been in Japan for a week preparing for what is my biggest test in my still young international career. Everything was going well until, five weeks earlier, I tore my adductor muscle at a low-key event in Loughborough. This has thrown me into great mental and physical confusion. I have become preoccupied with my technique, and with my preparation, which I am convinced are all wrong.

I am therefore using the last few days in Japan to try to stamp out this problem. On this particular day I go off to Chiba, a Tokyo suburb, with my coach, John Trower, and my British colleague, Mick Hill.

Three years later, with just one week to go before the start of the European Championships in Helsinki, I am in much better shape. My preparation has been interrupted again by another pulled adductor muscle, this time four weeks prior to the championships. This time, however, I know that I am in good shape, which means that I never question my fitness nor my preparation. I am enjoying a massage on the affected area, and resting the leg, giving it time to recover, and not panicking. I spend the next hour watching a video of my first ever world record throw, back in 1990, in Stockholm. I pay particular attention to the rhythms, timing and the run-up, so that by the end of the hour, I have something like one-hundred world-class throws in my mind.

Back in Chiba I am 90 minutes into a very hard training session. I have already completed a lot of throws but I just can't find the right position. Although the adductor is playing up, I have managed to throw 83 metres, which should have been seen as a respectable distance. But I want more. It is a sign of my lack of confidence that I feel it necessary to throw 85 metres in training in order to prove to myself that I am on track for the world title.

I fail to throw any further and, two days later, I am still in great pain as a result of the hammering I have given my body in training and throwing. It is now just 48 hours before the competition starts for real, but I am far from happy with the technical side of my throwing. I decide to go through a last-minute run-up session. I just want to see myself get it right before the World Championships begin but, 45 minutes into the session, I have still failed to find the answer, and I am growing increasingly desperate.

However, over in Helsinki, it is three days before the start of the competition, and I am off to the track with a very clear picture of my rhythm and technique in my mind because of the session I did with the videotape. My adductor has been relaxed, and has therefore recovered. I have not been paying too much attention in the last few days to any particular technical positions, preferring to focus on the whole picture. The actual training session is a long warm-up and stretch, followed by a couple of run-ups. I perform just two, enough to act out the rhythm in my mind.

For the last two days before the start of the competition, I am trying to take my mind away from the track. If there is any pre-competition visualizing to be done, it is purely on the rhythms. Twice a day, I have allocated an hour for very concentrated visualization. I am not questioning anything about my preparation, nor my technique. It leaves me in an extremely relaxed state.

This is in some contrast to my state of mind in Tokyo, where we return once again. I am still trying to find what I feel to be the correct position to deliver my longest throw. Whenever I decide on one, I then question and analyse it so much that before long I have too many doubts about it. The morning of the qualifying competition finally comes round and I am awake by 5.00 a.m., ready to start my bid to become world champion. Ninety minutes later, I am warming up at the track, and suddenly I feel a sense of confidence after throwing the javelin more than 75 metres after a very short run-up. This is great news. Maybe I have finally found the right formula, even at this late stage.

Meanwhile, in Helsinki, I am also at the warm-up area two hours before the start of the qualifying round. My goals in preparation for the actual competition are good rhythm and control, and I am achieving them during warm-up. I only perform one run-up, in order to simulate what I will do in the actual stadium. I am also completely uninterested in how far the javelin is flying.

Returning to Tokyo, I leave the warm-up area deciding that I will deal with the run-up when I come to it in the qualifying round. I believe I have enough in the bank to get through the morning, and providing I achieve this I feel I will then be well set for the final. After all, it has not really gone wrong in the past. After a further two warm-up throws in the stadium, I am ready to take my first throw for real. Walking back down the run-up, I turn to look down the field and suddenly think how long the run-up appears. The check marks on the track seem alien to me, and the scratch line, which I cannot cross, seems miles away. As a result, I approach my first throw in a very tentative manner, and record a useless throw. I know I have messed it up, but at least I have another two throws to salvage the situation. I spend the next half hour, while waiting for my next throw, watching the others perform.

Back in Helsinki, I qualify with my first-round throw, recording 81 metres, by enjoying a clear rhythm in my mind that I am then able to transfer onto the track. It is nothing special, but enough to get through and qualify for the day and the final, and that's what really matters.

Things back in Tokyo are fast progressing from bad to worse. My second throw was as bad as my first, and my third and final attempt is so desperate it all happens in a blur. For the last effort, I doubt myself so much that I choose a javelin I have never used before because I have just seen someone else throw it a long way.

The next day I was on my way home. A 10-hour flight gave me a chance to reflect on what had happened to me. I just could not comprehend the speed at which the previous 24 hours had passed. I seemed to be in a semi-sleepy state of mind, in which I just couldn't see clearly what had really gone wrong. I had been so engrossed in my problems that I did not attend to the job in hand – finding the right rhythm to throw the javelin – and as a result I was sitting on the plane while 12 members of the opposition were battling it out for a world championship title that I had been favourite to win.

Let's jump ahead again – to Helsinki and the day of the final. The details of how I had qualified had been forgotten and the whole episode, which seemed so important at the time, now just seemed like a simple stepping stone. Warming up for the final, I took a moment to assess my level of arousal, which I needed slightly to reduce, before focusing on the whole movement of jogging. Throughout the warm-up throws, I never lost sight of a very natural rhythm, and I was also very conscious not to get caught up in any pre-final competitions that would in no way seriously reflect on the actual final.

I paid very little attention to how far the javelin was travelling, instead I focused on how cleanly I was hitting the javelin, and on the various technical process skills I had identified along the way to this day. The result of all this was a big early throw, which not only placed everyone else under immediate pressure, but which eventually turned out to be too good for my opposition.

The big throw came about as a result of a massive rush of adrenaline, which caused excitement. I was able to convert this into a peak performance because I was in a relaxed state of mind, and this only came about because I had done my psychological homework. It was almost as if I was on autopilot, so that when I actually produced the throw good enough to make me the 1994 European champion, the whole movement came together, and it was as if I was watching someone else throw the javelin.

THEORY ....

Hopefully your preparation, both physically and mentally, is in place for the big day, but it can still go wrong on the one day that it really matters. For me, the ultimate competitors are those who can dig deepest on the day to the point of achieving a lifetime best, when it is asked of them, and not just when they feel up for it. Rarely do we know just how we are going to react to this ultimate challenge until we are actually confronted by it.

What we should be finding is the point of being totally engrossed in our own task, without any distraction or doubt in mind. This point is more likely to be achieved if we are prepared for it. But there are occasions, however, when we are asked to react purely to another person's actions. In a split second, we have to read the situation, analyse and process it, deciding upon and then executing the right response.

In order to carry this off, of course, we need to be in the right frame of mind, and once we have detected this, we then need to be able to reproduce it when required. In order to achieve this, we must pass through a few key phases.

The training begins at a very conscious level, as if we are learning a new skill. Our competence is therefore low. The next frame is to move from incompetence to a conscious level, still incompetent at the skill we are trying to develop, but consciously trying to do something about it.

The next step is to take this conscious incompetence and turn it into conscious competence, which will take up the second half of training and preparation. By the time you are required to compete to your optimum level on the big day of an actual competition, you are ultimately looking for a level of unconscious competence from which your performance naturally springs. In this state, you do not have to attend consciously to technical faults, and your competence is at a peak.

Timothy Gallwey provides the best explanation for this when he uses a theory that helped chop my golf handicap in half. His theory is based on the fact that inside our minds are two cells, almost two people. The first person, Self 1, is the voice inside us that is consciously assessing, analysing and instructing Self 2, the other person, who is very rhythmic and creative. When doubt creeps in, Self 1 is constantly reminding Self 2 of his mistakes. Self 1 doesn't really trust Self 2, and therefore constantly communicates with him in an attempt to take over. Gallwey goes on to say that when we perform optimally there is very little communication between Self 1 and 2, and, in fact, Self 2 is actually far more competent than Self 1. The key is therefore to have control over who we let dominate our movements. As I have just explained, it is unconscious competence that we ultimately want to use when competing, which is more characteristic of Self 2 than Self 1. But there is still a duty towards Self 1, both during the initial and intermediate preparation period, and, possibly, for those who are more skilled in the art of controlling Self 1 than Self 2 at a competition site, where Self 1 can act as our own internal coach.

My own adoption of this technique is very pronounced when it comes to golf. I have found that whenever I have been concerned with the position of my hands, my feet, my centre of gravity, or any small local movement in any of my joints, then the ultimate goal of striking the ball efficiently is impaired. In contrast, on other days, I have simply turned up at a golf course, hit a few balls and enjoyed the movement of swinging the club and watching the ball fly through the air. As a result, I have subsequently enjoyed a better round of golf by just working on the whole movement, rhythm and timing, while still drawing on both 'Selfs' at the same time.

This is all very well when it is going right, but when things begin to go wrong, the most natural reaction in the world is to question something, whether it is physical, mental or technical, and then, generally, to end up doubting ourselves. So how do we induce this Self 2 attitude and, more importantly, if we make a mistake, how do we prevent Self 1 from being too overpowering in its analysis, and instead focus again on Self 2?

As an accomplished tennis player, Gallwey came up with what he refers to as the 'bounce-hit' method in his own game, which we have already mentioned earlier in the book. The practice would be to say 'bounce' as the ball bounced, and to say 'hit' as you hit the ball. By saying these two words during play, you are actually performing the skill of hitting the ball with the racquet, and not thinking about it. What he found was that people improved the timing in their stroke play by carrying out his theory, and thereby improved the actual strokes. There was an improvement in coordination, in balance, in control and consistency so that, eventually, all the factors made for a much better tennis player.

You can do the same thing in golf, of course. Say 'Back' at the end of your back swing, and 'Hit' as you strike the ball, again taking away all of the unnecessary information, which, on the big day, could impair your timing and control.

My own version of this is comparing it to what makes up a song – the lyrics and the tune. If we just speak the words of a song, a few people might recognize it, but if we were to sing the same words to the right tune, most people would recognize it. For me, simply learning the positions of a technique in our given discipline without rhythmically tying them together is the same as speaking the words of a song. The tune is far more recognizable and has far greater potential to portray the correct series of motions, and it is therefore the theme that we should be paying most attention to when learning a skill.

I remember when the press kept asking me what had gone wrong, after I had failed even to qualify for the 1991 World Championships final. The answer that came to my mind back then was that I just could not hear the music. It seemed to sum up what had been missing for me that day, and since then a lot of my training has been based around learning the tune that will accompany my event, alongside the technical positions.

But how do we find this tune? I believe the easiest way to do this is either to copy someone else who has a good rhythm and who is a more proficient performer, or by taking your best day and remembering how you felt on that day. If you happen to have it on video, then you can actually see the rhythm. It is then possible to transcribe this onto an audio tape, listen to the rhythms of your feet and hands, and actually hear the rhythm, or the music, if you like, of your event. This will enhance your visualization, providing your rhythm is running at normal time.

Hopefully, by the time you have come to compete, you have

combined several people's rhythms into one big picture, which will predominantly include your own. This becomes a totally unique picture. It exists only in your mind. Nobody else has exactly the same picture.

I cannot stress enough the importance of visualization at the competition site itself. Where subtle technical changes can be the crux of the sport, why waste time and energy by actually trying them out and performing them, a task that may be impractical during the competition, when they can simply be viewed in your mind's eye. Reinforcement of this position, incorporating all of your process goals, is a fundamental aspect when it comes to performing at optimum level.

If all else fails on the big day of performance, and if you are effectively choking and questioning your ability, Self 1 has clearly taken over; you are analysing yourself to the point of being destructive. If you go back and accept that you know that your rhythm is correct, then you will still understand your tune. By this stage, the breakdown of your technique must be unconscious, and the rhythms should have taken over; Self 2 should be playing the more important role.

Your tune, or your rhythm, is the most important factor, and can only be found in Self 2. Putting Self 1 to one side is a skill in itself. This is achieved by continually diverting your attention away from Self 1 at the competition site. We must, however, bear in mind that Self 1 plays an integral part in our ability to prepare effectively. The real skill is in being able to call upon these different modes of analysis, when needs be, while also being able to perform fluently during competition, which is what we should all strive to do. The ultimate is to train Self 1 to be present and observant, but quiet, so as to let Self 2 continue uninterrupted.

One other important element of competition is being able to perform while suffering from an injury. It is not what any sportsperson wants, but it is often the case that he or she will find ways of overcoming such a potential problem, rather than just withdrawing, particularly if it is an event that they have trained and prepared for, for quite some time.

My own personal experience of this, where I feel I carried this of to great effect, was at the 1991 World Student Games in Sheffield. Despite suffering from a torn adductor muscle, acquired in an injury a month before, I was still able to come through and win the Gold Medal.

During my warm-up phase, I couldn't help but be aware of pain in the upper half of my right leg. I went through a phase of questioning whether I should actually be competing at all, but I managed to turn my negative thoughts round by telling myself that the top half of my body was in very good shape, and I was still able to generate a great deal of force in training. It was this that I then focused on during the competition, rather than my injury.

My advice to you in such a situation would be to emphasize whatever is good about your ability to perform. By focusing on this, it will not only give you the confidence to perform, it will also divert your attention away from the problem area.

SUMMARY

It seems to be, judging by the two 'Groundhog Day' examples portrayed in the story section of this chapter, that a prerequisite to winning is to not analyse nor question your performance continuously. If you have carried out your homework correctly, then you should be able to avoid the temptation. There should be no stones left unturned in your training and preparation for the big day, and if you have identified and met all your goals, as well as visualized what is about to take place for real, then there should be no surprises.

When you know everything about the big day ahead of you, then you should be able to carry out much of the day unconsciously. At the competition site, it is necessary to become less conscious but more focused in order to capture tunnel vision. Knowing that everything has been done can only instill confidence, which will breed relaxation, which, in turn, will allow you to perform optimally. All this goes back to the arousal theory, which underlines again how every strand of sports psychology is linked.

The story is designed to show that, even though all your preparation may have been thorough, your state of mind in the last few days and on the actual day itself can prove to be the crucial factor behind success or failure. Winning always starts with your state of mind, and even though it has been in good shape all the way through your training and preparation, it can still trip you up on the big day. It is, if you like, a bit like a football team. They may try their hardest for 89 minutes of a game, but if they suddenly decide they can't be bothered to play for the last 60 seconds, the chances are that they will concede a goal. By understanding what our mind is up to around and on the big day, we are much less likely to be tricked.

I made several fundamental mistakes in Tokyo that I did not make in Helsinki, and there is clearly a pretty fine line between the two. I could easily have made exactly the same mistakes in Helsinki as I did at the 1991 World Championships because the cues for falling into the trap were exactly the same. However drastic the difference between coming fifteenth in 1991, and first in 1994, there is a fine line that you can, by manipulating your psychological make-up, overcome.

With the benefit of glorious hindsight, I can now see that one of my first mistakes back in 1991 was that my visualization had been very scratchy as a result of my doubts. This doubt was borne out of a lack of confidence, which quickly spiralled downwards. The second mistake was to try to turn it around by working on the analytical side of my brain, trying to satisfy and pamper my Self 2. I told myself I wanted five good-quality throwing sessions, and I was trying, physically, to turn around my lack of confidence. I analysed myself 24 hours a day and became preoccupied with my problems.

By doing this, I then created a further physical problem, because nobody in their right mind, if seriously intending to win a global title, should carry out five full training sessions in the fortnight before the competition – at least not in my discipline.

It would have been very easy to have slid down the same spiral in Helsinki after hurting myself again, but this time I told myself that I was in good shape because my preparation had

Above: I may look pretty lonely and depressed, but in fact I am simply concentrating as hard as I can on visualizing my next throw, step by step, movement by movement, so that when the moment comes I will simply be performing a sequence of actions I have already thoroughly rehearsed in my mind. ALLSPORT

Left: And you never feel better than when the performance goes exactly as rehearsed! MARK SHEARMAN

Two very different players with two very different ways of relaxing – John McEnroe (left) and Bjorn Borg (right) each do their own thing. ALLSPORT

When a championship depends on a single shot even the most experienced sportsperson can run into trouble: Steve Davis (left) and Dennis Taylor (right) look anything but relaxed during their critical, final frame in the 1985 World Snooker Championships. ALLSPORT

Training can be very hard work indeed and only those who keep their goals clearly in mind through the long winter months can expect success in the coming season. MARK SHEARMAN

Left: A moment Bernhard Langer will probably never forget – the fatal misputt at the end of the 1991 Ryder Cup.
ALLSPORT

Below: Nick Faldo, the player who had the courage to take his swing apart and start from scratch; he was rewarded with even greater success. ALLSPORT

Two leading British athletes who have put the lessons of sports psychology into practice.

Jonathan Edwards, Britain's world champion triple jumper has described how he achieved his goal of 'just jumping into the sand-pit'. ALLSPORT

Linford Christie is a model of concentration in the last crucial few moments before the start of a sprint. You could set a bomb off next to him and he would never even notice it. MARK SHEARMAN

The Europa Cup at Gateshead in 1989 was the first time I had been part of a British team, and the first time I realized the real 'lift' that an athlete can get from sharing a common goal with fellow team members. ALLSPORT

It was Kriss Akabusi who set the team up for victory at Gateshead by winning the very first event, the 400 metres hurdles. MARK SHEARMAN

Even for an athlete who, like myself, competes in individual events, it is essential to recognize that you are part of a team, and no-one is a more important member of my team than my coach. John Trower, on this occasion at least, was evidently equally pleased with the results of our teamwork. ALLSPORT

This photograph taken at Helsinki in 1994 gives some impression of what a javelin thrower feels like when he stands poised to begin his run-up at a major event. Nothing can quite prepare you for the experience of facing a crowd of thousands for the first time – as I found out at the World Junior Championships in Canada in 1988. MARK SHEARMAN been better, I had set myself proper goals, and had used visualization well. It meant that instead of training even harder, and running my body down, in an attempt to clear up my mental and physical problems, I was able to relax and rest, but still give my full attention to finding the rhythm needed to win the European Gold Medal.

The next mistake in Tokyo was that I set myself unrealistic goals. I had thrown 83 metres in training, but I wanted more. By trying to get 110 per cent out of myself, I only succeeded in placing a huge amount of physical stress on my body. This, of course, could only result in more physical problems.

Last minute changes proved to be the next crucial error in this catalogue of mistakes in Tokyo. The day before the qualifying competition began, I was trying to make late changes to my run-ups, rather like panic revision for an exam at school the following morning. It just does not work.

In contrast, in Helsinki, I got it right. Through good visualization sessions, I was able to see exactly what I needed to do to meet my outcome goals, and therefore when I hurt myself, it failed to blur my vision. The physical training sessions were a great deal shorter, which obviously limited the stress and toll on my body. Only the necessary questions were asked, which restricted how far I was prepared to allow Self 1 to have a say in matters. I had the confidence to dispel the unrealistic doubts that were creeping into my psyche, courtesy of Self 1, and I therefore prevented him from wrecking my chances of success.

I clearly failed to do this in Tokyo. Instead, Self 1 took complete control, and proved to be the cause behind my desperate and increasingly erratic search for a correct position. This, in turn, manifested itself in an unrealistic perception of time. If you ever experience this, then you must instantly recognize that this is one of the cues for letting you know that events are not going well. Things are happening far too quickly, and this is when you should stop, slow down and regroup. But I did not recognize this. All of a sudden, I was finding comfort in the fact that I could throw 75 metres of a short run-up. The fact that this did not equate to coming off my full run in the stadium in order to throw 83 metres-plus did not seem to bother me.

The next factor in my contrasting fortunes of 1991 and 1994 was that, in Helsinki, it was my rhythm and point control that proved to be the key elements in the warm-up. I wasn't looking for external reassurances in terms of distance, but rather an internal confidence that my rhythm would be correct. I allowed myself to fall into what I had been seeing for many weeks. Doing what I had been seeing became a natural progression. As a result, Helsinki became a stroll in the park because I was merely repeating what I had already seen thousands of times before.

While the event in Helsinki *seemed* to take as long as it did in reality, back in Tokyo the 90-minute qualifying competition seemed to flash past in about 10 minutes flat. A desperately false perception of time forced me to rush at attempting to salvage the disastrous mental and physical state I had allowed myself to fall into. I may have been the European and Commonwealth champion, but I can now recognize that, in such a state, I was never going to win the world title.

What a contrast, though, in Helsinki. I stepped up for the second-round throw in the final feeling incredibly excited at the prospect, and knowing that a big throw was on. My first-round throw had given me this clue, and if I want to be really harsh on myself, perhaps I should have produced the big one with my first-round effort. But I had another chance, and, this time, I took it. My unconscious competence ensured a winning throw.

It seems a lot to ask of yourself to put in so much mental effort before an event, only then to be expected to work just as hard on the big day. But nothing is guaranteed, especially when the big day finally comes round, and it would be an even greater shame if you had put in all the required mental work beforehand, only to let slip at the eleventh hour, and undo all the good work. This is why the competition element of psychology is so important, because in my game, and with the standards I have set for myself, you need to complete the job.

I should emphasize how thin I believe the line is between achieving your optimum level and not achieving it. How many times do people seem capable of achieving their given task, only to fail to fulfil their potential on the day. Therefore, what could be perceived to be a very small change in psychological preparation is likely to have a very large effect on the outcome of a performance.

Once the outcome is clear, you then need to attribute success or failure. If you do not know how to do this, then you will never learn from your mistakes, which would make any experience worthless. Remember, as so many people both in sport and in other areas have said, the most successful are those who have failed first, and then learnt. This is where the attribution stage of psychology comes into play.

8. ATTRIBUTION

· ·

So now it's all over. After all the planning, training and preparation, the event has suddenly passed by, leaving you feeling anything from a glowing sense of achievement, to a miserable sense of failure. Whatever happens, it's too late now.

Well, actually, this is only partly true. Yes, it may be too late to salvage the particular event that has just passed, but what about the next occasion? Surely, you can gain something from your experience, even if it was a miserable one?

This is where attribution pays such an important part. If you learn how to attribute correctly, then you stand much more of a chance of turning your initial failure into success, or ensuring that you continue to succeed.

STORY ....

In the last chapter, my story centred on what I consider to be the worst moment of my career, the 1991 World Championships, where I failed even to qualify for the final. I am going to continue to use this particular case to underline the part attribution plays in my life and, indeed, in yours.

As I launched my third, and final effort in the qualifying stage of the Tokyo World Championships, I knew instantly that I had inexplicably failed to meet the required mark of 82 metres, a length that I could normally produce standing on my head. As the javelin flew through the air my hands went up to my head as I stood and watched in disbelief.

....

The disastrous thought of failure had already hit me before that final effort. The fact that I was contemplating doom and disaster was probably a contributing factor towards my poor third throw. Even before I had finished, I was finding reasons for, or attributing towards, my failure.

I started to introduce what are classed as external factors behind the disaster. It was only 9.00a.m. in the morning – that must have been the reason. Then again, maybe I was ill. It got a lot worse after that final throw when I realized that I was not going to feature in a final that most people expected me to win.

My immediate reaction then was to tell myself that someone must have drugged me. I thought about the cup of coffee I had earlier that morning. Maybe someone had done something to the coffee? After all, I hadn't thrown 78 metres, which was the distance recorded for my last throw, for many years. Almost every time I went out to throw I was getting closer to 88 metres, but here I was throwing 78 metres.

Then I started to look around, trying to see if I could blame the wind. No, there was very little breeze at all. What about the temperature? Was it too hot, or too humid? As I packed my bag and started to walk out of the stadium, I could not get out of there quick enough. If there had been a large enough stone lying around, I would have curled up underneath it. The walk from the centre of the stadium to the bus took only 10 minutes, but it seemed like an hour. To this day, it remains an extremely vivid picture. I can even remember what Jan Zelezny, who also experienced an equally strange failure, was wearing.

During that walk I was wondering how I was going to explain myself to my friends and family, my coach and the media, who were all waiting for me. It occurred to me that this was the first time I had completely failed. It was a new experience, and I became obsessed with trying to find out why it had happened. I needed a reason, because without one I couldn't account for my shock result.

I also went through just about every emotion possible during that walk. First came the embarrassment. I told myself that everyone was looking at me, pointing their fingers at the failure. I suddenly felt extremely self-conscious, as if I was standing out, but for all the wrong reasons.

The next stage was to tell myself that the failure hadn't actually happened. I did this by shrugging my shoulders, holding my hands up in the air and almost laughing about it. It was an attempt, I suppose, to hide what had just happened.

This, however, is one of the good aspects of athletics. You can't get away with this. The result is there for everyone to see, and you have to face up to your performance, whether you win, lose or draw. You then realize that this dismissive response is just another emotional stage.

The next emotion generates the need and the desire to find the reason behind your performance. This is the longest step, and I believe that until you have successfully attributed what you have just done, you will never get over it, move on and put it all behind you.

If there is one thing you can guarantee it is that you can't change the past. By saying this to yourself, it is another step towards recovering from the series of events. I went through a list of every possibility and eventuality, until I eventually realized that, for example, the milk on my cereal that morning would not have made any difference to my performance.

By the end of the walk, I was beginning to work out that I was fast running out of things I could blame my failure on. It is the most natural thing in the world to attempt to find anything or anyone to blame except for yourself. But, forced by this discovery, I reluctantly turned my attention towards myself. The next process was to start questioning myself.

To get to the bottom of my failure, I had to address every factor, which included wondering whether, on that day, I was physically capable of throwing 80 metres. I had a small adductor injury, but I had thrown 83 metres in training the week before, so I reckoned that I was perfectly capable of producing the required distance.

My second question was, did I have bad luck? Again, the answer was a definite 'no'. Javelin throwing, in my opinion, never boils down to luck. After analysing if I was asking too much of myself physically, which was slightly different to the first question, I then moved on to whether I had tried too hard?

Well, maybe I had. I started to pursue this particular avenue as I walked towards the waiting press, who all wanted to know what had gone so wrong.

Yes, I had tried too hard and I had let the pressure get to me. If I was going to be brutally honest about it, I had choked. There, I had finally admitted it. It took a while coming, but at last it came out. The effect of this choking was that I failed to find any rhythm in the run-up, hence my substandard throwing.

As I walked up to the press, I could see the disbelief on their faces. Eventually someone asked the big question: 'What happened?' As I explained in the previous chapter, I told them that I just couldn't hear the music. After seeing their puzzled expressions, I elaborated, explaining that I lost all rhythm on the runway, but I didn't actually admit to choking, because that would have been exceptionally hard on myself.

As I walked away, I consoled myself that I would do everything in my powers to ensure that it would never happen again. If there was going to be anything positive to be taken from this experience it was that I was going to learn from it and use it as a tool in the future.

The next person I had to confront was my coach, John Trower. I remember trying to find him in the Tokyo crowd during the qualifying session for reassurance. He could see that everything was wrong while I was throwing. I couldn't pull the wool over his eyes because he knew I was in good enough shape. I could see the frustration and disappointment in his face. I could have gone to the press and said I had an injury. I didn't, of course, but I could have done. But there was no way I could have got away with that with John. It was a hard thing to admit to John, but I told him I had messed up. That, at last, was all there was to say on the matter – at least at that time.

To try and remove the frustration, I then went over to some nearby baseball pitching nets. I think I actually pushed someone out of the way and stomped straight to the front of the queue with a bucket of baseballs. I'm not very proud of that, but I suppose it showed how I was feeling.

The nets actually measure the speed the baseballs are travelling, which, in my case, was 120 mph. All this exercise achieved was to add to my frustration, because by pitching the balls at great speed, it confirmed that there was nothing physically wrong with me. As I walked away, I realized that this was the case. I had just messed up, and it had all been in the head. I could probably have walked back into the stadium and thrown 88 metres but, of course, it was all too late.

Jumping back onto the bus, my frustration turned to anger. When I finally reached my hotel room and closed the door behind me, it was the first time I had been completely alone with my thoughts. Four hours earlier, I had left that same room, with my bag packed, the thought of failing to qualify never even having crossed my mind. Realizing what I had done and, worse still, how I had done it, was a terrible moment. In anger, I threw half my kit out of the window. Thankfully, the area below was a closed-off area, otherwise my kit, from 13 floors up, could have caused some damage. My trainers, incidentally, landed on another roof right across the street. It was the best throw I had produced that morning.

The next few days, and the flight home, were hard to deal with, but at least I had the chance to make amends at the big, post-World Championships meeting at Sheffield a fortnight later. The top 20 javelin throwers in the world would be there, and I saw this as my chance to tell them that I was still the best in the world, even if I had mucked it up at the World Championships.

This time, I performed in the way I had always known I was capable of, winning the competition with a throw of 91.36 metres, which broke my own British and Commonwealth record. As I walked away, my initial response was that I had answered back in the best possible way, but then, after just a few seconds, I realized what Sheffield was really telling me: that, mentally, I had failed two weeks previously in Tokyo. It certainly dispelled any thoughts I might have been harbouring that it could have been down to physical reasons. It simply underlined the fact that the physical doubts I had around the Tokyo Games were actually mental, reminding me of the inextricable link between mind and body.

My physical condition that day was pretty much the same as

it was in Tokyo, but the difference was my rhythm, which was created by a sound, mental state. Any thought of trying to attribute my failure to external reasons was eradicated by my ability physically to discount them at Sheffield.

As the winter of 1991 drew on, it was the motivation of proving my mental ability that focused a great deal of my energy. Rhythm, in particular, was underlined 50 times in my mind as a crucial part of my training. It was while I was in New Zealand, in the early part of 1992, that this led to a new world record of 91.46 metres.

Just as I had attributed my failure in Tokyo during the summer, I also needed to attribute my success in setting a new world best mark. The external factors were good: it was windy and warm. But there was more to it than that. I wasn't going to put it down to luck, especially as it was only January, an unusual time of the year to break a world record. In the end, just as the main reason for failing in Tokyo was the lack of rhythm, I attributed this throw to finding the right rhythm.

THEORY ....

The whole point of this chapter is that you must attribute correctly in order to learn from your mistakes and make the necessary amendments to your mental and physical performance. Thelma S. Horn, in her book *The Advantage of Sports Psychology*, says: 'The attribution theory is concerned with how individuals appraise the outcomes of achievement situations.' We are therefore concerned with who, or what, we must blame if we have performed badly, or who, or what we must attribute the success to in terms of achievement.

If we are successfully to assess our performance so that we can move on and quickly improve our performance, it is important that we first understand the theory behind attribution in order to reduce the chances of repeating our mistakes. The biggest mistake would be to attribute a failure to the wrong reason week after week. I've done this in the past by gearing my training around preventing what I *thought* were the reasons for my failure, and so merely wasted time adapting my training to areas that weren't affecting my initial performance.

The attribution theory has an endless list of factors, but I wish to highlight four particular elements, which Bernard Weiner first identified in 1972: first, our ability; second, the effort we put in; third, the difficulty of the task; and fourth, sheer luck.

It is important to decide not only which factor applies, but also whether the factor is external or internal. In other words, was your performance down to you, for reasons created by you, or was it down to something out of your control?

It is very common to hear a sportsperson who has just failed attributing their performance to an external problem. It was too cold, it was raining, they were kept waiting, or whatever the case may be. What fascinates me is how so many of them attribute failure to external reasons, but attribute success to their level of skill, their ability to handle pressure, or their strength of mind.

It all boils down to confidence. When you hear people say that they had done brilliantly that day because they were very skilful you would immediately think that, at the very least, they were extremely confident. In my opinion, from a psychological viewpoint, it is fine to admit this, providing they are prepared also to admit that their failures too are down to their lack of skill, or the fact that they choked or, for that matter, any other internal factor.

Weiner referred to the ability to learn from mistakes as 'attribution dependency'. His studies highlighted the 'feel-good factor'. Basically, when you succeed and achieve, you obviously feel that everything is great. Alternatively, when you fail, you should be feeling pretty bad about the whole state of affairs. This, in turn, creates a desire to search for answers as to why the particular outcome occurred.

Expectation and reaction are the keys to establishing a stable and consistent pattern to our behaviour. To help us assess our outcome we need to focus once again on our process goals, which we outlined in the chapter geared towards goal-setting. For any given competition or training session we could have a number of process goals, but we need to assess each one of them to help us explain how the outcome, whether satisfactory, or disappointing, was eventually reached.

For example, if a golfer stands on a tee, hooks his ball out of bounds, and then does not break down his attribution into process skills, he will not be able to recognize where he went wrong, and is more than likely to repeat the shot next time. If, however, he can attribute his poor shot to finishing his back swing early, he can then attend to this technical problem, and hit the next drive straight down the middle of the fairway.

For an individual sport, such as golf, accepting responsibility for your own performance is almost a prerequisite to playing the game. There are many other cases, however, where people have tremendous difficulty accepting responsibility for their behaviour because they believe they have to be perfect. To them, anything less than perfect means failure. They, therefore, place the blame for any failure on external factors in order not to tarnish their feeling of striving for perfection.

Eventually, such a person will develop a lack of confidence, because there are only two ways to react to this: either blaming others, or becoming convinced of being no good. By removing this desire to be perfect, and instead determining to do our best in every situation immediately gives a sense of decreased pressure.

Instead of constantly searching and questioning – which can only be destructive – consistent improvement can be guaranteed if you merely strive to improve on your best. I used to be one of those people who insisted that perfection was the only way forward, but now I realize that this philosophy will inevitably lead to an unhappy existence, because the vast majority of the time this merely invites unwanted and unnecessary pressure. Until that one-in-a-million day when you hit ultimate perfection, nothing else will ever provide contentment, because you haven't quite reached your goal, even if you have won the competition.

It is easy to fall into the trap of striving for perfection, which is usually generated by the expectations of parents, friends and trainers, but time and time again, this need to be perfect messes up the psyche, particularly that of a child. All you will do is learn to attribute your failures to external factors and therefore convince yourself that you have no internal weaknesses, even if you do keep on failing each time.

Of course, there will be genuine occasions when an external factor can work against you. A bad call, for example, in a tennis game will lose you a point you should have won. Very often, such an occasion, particularly at an event such as Wimbledon, will lead to a loss in concentration, and therefore to the loss of further points. The classic example of this happened in 1993, when Jana Novotna seized defeat from the jaws of victory against Steffi Graf in the ladies' singles final. Leading 4–1 in the final set, and 40–30, she produced a double fault to level the score in the game to deuce. This error affected her mental state so badly that she went on to lose the match in tears. But what proper attribution should teach you is to accept that you have just experienced a piece of bad luck, and then turn it around by increasing your focus and winning the next few points.

After all, you cannot change the sequence of events that have just taken place, but you can change the way you react to them, by accepting that while there is nothing you can do about the external factors, there is everything you can do about controlling the internal ones.

SUMMARY ....

It is easy after performing to assess your display on the outcome in an objective sport such as athletics. In my event, the javelin, you receive a distance. In another sports event, like gymnastics, you receive a score. In business, you might meet a certain sales target. These are the outcome goals.

The importance of turning these outcome goals back into process goals cannot be stressed enough. If you can look back and honestly assess your process goals, then you should be able to discover where, if it is the case, you went wrong. It is common for an accomplished golfer, for example, to tear his game apart having just won a tournament. He did okay, but his putting was terrible on the final nine holes, or his swing didn't feel as good today. What he is actually doing is marking his process goals, on a scale of one to ten, if you like. The fact that he won therefore becomes irrelevant. He clearly performed well enough to beat the rest of the field, but it may well be that he could only give himself a mark of seven out of ten for his putting, and eight out of ten for his approach shots.

Nick Faldo is perhaps the best example here. Despite enjoying huge success as one of the world's top golfers, he decided, with the help of the top golf coach, David Leadbetter, totally to dismantle his swing, which, obviously, is one of the most crucial strokes in the game. He clearly decided that, although he had done well in the past, his swing was recording a modest number on his personal wagon wheel scale. There was room for improvement here, hence his seemingly radical action. The result, however, was even greater success, and a host of major titles.

It is the trait of almost every top sportsperson I know, that they are never satisfied. Whatever they may have achieved, there is always room for improvement. If this were not the case, then they may as well retire from their sport and find a new challenge. It is therefore good practice to reassess constantly and shuffle around your process goals in training and competition to give yourself a specific goal, and after performing it, assess it. I gave myself nine out of ten the other day for a weight-training session in which I was able to implement a specific movement for the first time and make it an effective part of the overall lift. In contrast, while performing a bounding session (which is where I improve the power in my upper legs by jumping up steps in a sports stadium), my focus was poor and I could, therefore, only give myself six out of ten. These were the best and worst sessions from a typical week's training, and the following week my goal was to perform each session at a minimum of seven out of ten.

The story in this chapter outlined my process of attribution, following firstly what I consider to be my biggest failure, and then, within a few months, one of my major successes. This confirmed to me how relatively unimportant my perceived physical well-being is, in comparison to my mental state, in the physical sport in which I compete.

Although it may have taken a little while for me to realize it, I attributed both my huge disappointment in Tokyo and my world record throw in New Zealand to the same element of my throwing – the rhythm on the run-up. I simply got it dead right on one occasion, and terribly wrong on the other. Although I tried hard to find an external reason, physical elements did not really come into it. It highlighted, if you like, the thin line between success and failure. Looking at it from a scale point of view, I would give my rhythm two out of ten in Tokyo, and nine out of ten in New Zealand.

Rhythm is therefore a key part of my fortunes in athletics. As a result, the sports psychologist, Dave Collins, who is working with me, has introduced me to some techniques that are geared towards ensuring a good rhythm each time I throw. We have taken a few examples of my best throws, both in length and in technical and rhythmical terms, for example, my world record in Stockholm, and transcribed the video footage of these throws. We have then digitized the foot contacts onto audio tape, giving them one kind of bleep for my left foot, and a slightly different-sounding bleep for my right foot. The idea is that the bleeps will provide audio proof of how rhythmical my throwing is. All I then have to do is keep on playing it, visualizing what is a good rhythmical throw, until it becomes second nature to me.

Do not be surprised, therefore, if you find that the reason you lost a tennis match one week, but beat the same fellow the next week, is centred on exactly the same element of your game, produced well or poorly, depending on your state of mind. Whatever the case, be honest with yourself.

In the story, my first reaction to, and explanation for, my failure was that someone must have drugged me. It was a ridiculous thought, and totally irrational, but the last person I wanted to blame was myself. No, there had to be an external reason. I then went through a check list of external factors, each time realizing that none of them was to blame. This process is valid, because you need to prove to yourself that the wind, or the rain, or whatever the potential cause might be, is not the real cause for failure. In the end, you know only too well that the finger must point at yourself.

Once you have then attributed the correct reason for the failure, you are then able to go to work on ensuring that it will never happen again. In my case, I could have argued that the mental problems and attitude did not stem from nothing, but because I was injured prior to the qualifying round. I hadn't before had the experience of injury, and this lack of experience meant that an injury, an external factor, prompted the far more dangerous mental, or internal, reaction.

So hold your hands up, look at yourself in the mirror, and tell the truth. If you can do this, then you are halfway to solving your problems. Then make sure you discover the correct reason for your success or failure, and work on it.

9. TEAMWORK

....

Throughout chapters two to eight, I have discussed using various aspects of psychology to better your chances of a peak performance in an individual scenario. On the face of it, the following chapter suggests that the use of your mind is probably less relevant because you are working with others.

Well, as you have discovered in other areas of this book, the mind still plays a crucial role, even in an area where you might possibly think otherwise. Although teamwork is about helping yourself and others raise performance levels for mutual benefit, the individual aspects of a correct mental state still achieve the eventual goal.

STORY ....

In the following examples the fact that 'teamwork' is often nothing more than a welcome addition to, and a motivating factor for, an individual performance, which, as a result, benefits the team, is highlighted. I know of few people in sport who are out-and-out team players. Of course, they always want the team they are a part of to succeed, but each believes that the best way for such collective success is through each individual striving to perform to the optimum level and, in some cases, trying to outdo one another.

The first time I was ever selected to compete in a British athletics team was back in 1985. The memory of representing my country, even if it was at school level, remains a vivid one, probably because it was my first experience of what I saw as a rarity in an individual sport such as athletics – teamwork.

We were going to compete in Dublin, and I remember turning up at the airport without knowing anyone else in the England team. At that moment I had no feeling of being part of any team, and viewed the whole affair as just another competition; I would throw my javelin and go home again.

But it began to change on the morning we all met at the airport, the day before the actual competition. I began to feel as though we all had a common purpose, and that seemed immediately to bond us as a team. For a start, we had a team meeting, which, for me, was a new concept. Every athlete in the team, no matter what event he or she was competing in, was present for the briefing. We were told what to expect as a collective group, and how proud we should feel by putting on the English vest. I particularly remember one member of the senior management explaining what it actually means to wear the vest and walk out into the stadium.

It did the trick for me. I instantly felt a rush of adrenaline just thinking about the prospect of being part of the England team. Suddenly, in that room, there developed a close affinity between the team members, regardless of what event they may have been specializing in. I cast my mind back to when I was younger, when my mind would fill with awe watching great athletes like Sebastian Coe and Steve Ovett competing in the British vest; that I was now part of the same team filled me with confidence

The meeting was then broken down into various discipline groups, where we continued our discussions in a smaller and more constructive way, which allowed us to air our views and enjoy personal communication with the team management. We were then reintroduced to the whole team, and the powerful message about representing my country was hammered out again.

An individual rep was then appointed to iron out any difficulties that I might encounter throughout the championships. This, too, was a new and welcoming experience for me, in total contrast to the usual feeling that, as an individual, it was all down to me to go out and perform.

There were two javelin throwers in the English team, myself and an athlete called Paul Bushnell, who, at the time, was slightly more accomplished at the event. After warming up we were both given a final talk by the team management, who pointed out that they did not care who beat who in the javelin competition, as long as it ensured that we finished first and second in the overall event, which would achieve maximum points for England. My task was, obviously, to finish in the top two. I would have done well to have beaten Bushnell in those days, but by working together during the competition, and fending each other off, it enabled him to win the event, and me to end up in second place. With mission accomplished we, together with the rest of the England team, enjoyed a party that night in which we all got to know each other a little more.

The next time I remember experiencing such a strong sense of team morale was during the Europa and World Cup competitions in 1989. This was the time when the British team was beginning to make huge inroads into the domination of world athletics by the traditional powers from the eastern bloc. The British team were by no means favourites to win the Europa Cup at Gateshead that year, but I remember feeling the same surge of confidence as I did during my first English schools' international match when I walked out into the stadium with a GB tracksuit on my back. I wasn't really known at the time, but the crowd's reaction to seeing a British athlete about to lock horns with the best from Europe made me feel very conscious of the fact that, once again, I was representing my country. As I warmed up I also became conscious of the fact that there was an added sense of expectancy to achieve because of the team points required.

It was something I did not enjoy at first because my initial translation of this was tension, which, by increasing stress, was obviously a negative point. But during the warm-up, this tension was replaced by a sudden surge of motivation. As mine was one of the earlier events to take place, and because a javelin competition obviously takes longer to complete than most other disciplines, I could not help but let my attention wander to what else was going on inside the stadium during my own warm-up.

A particular roar from the crowd diverted my attention from my own task. Looking up, I could see that the athletes in the 400 metres hurdles, the Europa Cup's first competition, were cruising down the back straight. Kriss Akabusi was representing Great Britain and, as the athletes ran the second bend, with just over 100 metres remaining, Kriss moved into a position where he was capable of winning.

To say that the stadium's roof lifted is almost an understatement. The crowd went berserk as Kriss came in to win the first race, giving Britain an instant lead in the competition. Kriss wasn't expected to win. Indeed, we weren't expected to win the Europa Cup. We had never done so before, and we were up against the might of the Russians and the then dual powers of East and West Germany. But it proved to be a crucial moment for the team, and for me.

It was the first time I had ever experienced such an enthusiastic crowd and it lifted me to see another British athlete, and team-mate, performing so well on both his and my behalf. This lift rapidly translated into enthusiasm and motivation and I found that my next few warm-up throws were all 5 metres further in length.

Even now I find it amazing how powerfully someone else's performance within my team could influence me. As a result, I went on to win the javelin competition, my first major senior title, and enjoyed a similarly ecstatic reception from a very partisan crowd. We all shared a sense that something very special was in the process of happening. It was as if every single athlete in the team was lifted by each other's performances. The next day, the British team secured its first ever Europa Cup title, amid memorable scenes.

The other team I have benefited from enormously takes the shape of the back-up behind every top athlete these days. In the build-up to the Olympics, I will be using a whole host of people to help me prepare in the best possible way. These people include: a sports psychologist, a masseur, a physiotherapist, a kinesiologist, my coach, John Trower, and even my father, John, whom I always turn to for general advice.

Although different from, say, the GB Europa Cup team in format and goals, because this back-up team is there to enhance an individual's chances of success, it nevertheless can be classed as teamwork. Team Backley is really constructed of a series of partnerships, between myself and my coach, myself and my physio, myself and my psychologist, and so on, all of which become small teams in themselves. They sometimes interrelate with each other, and they all work towards the same goal: an Olympic Gold Medal at the Atlanta Games. We have worked together, in various shapes and guises, throughout my other achievements in international athletics, and all seem more than happy with the potentially uncomfortable fact that if I achieve success, it seems to be me who inevitably enjoys the spotlight and the glory far more than the rest of my team, who all helped to make it possible.

Still, I suppose it works the other way as well. At least they did not all get it in the neck like I did after my now well-chronicled failures!

THEORY ....

Let's take a closer look at the team behind me, as introduced above, in order to help our understanding of the relevance of teamwork to an individual performer. In all, a group of six people work with me, focusing on the same outcome goal. Although we all have our own, individual briefs, they are all stepping stones towards the outcome goal, and, therefore, we all need to be interreliant. The masseur and physio, for example, know each other, and therefore each other's work. This makes them aware of the other aspects of work being applied to my preparations, which produces a cohesion within the team. As I am the only one who could collect the Gold Medal, I am, if you like, the team leader, but success would not be possible without each and every member of the back-up team.

It is not that much different from explaining how Alan Shearer puts the ball in the back of the net. The beginning of that particular outcome is found three or four passes further down the line, perhaps even on the back of a substitution decision by the manager. On second thoughts, the process towards Shearer scoring that goal may have begun three months previously, with the work of a physiotherapist or psychologist to get him onto the pitch in the first place.

All have to be given credit in the process of achieving the outcome goal. I may be the one, if you like, who puts the ball in the back of the net. The result, between Shearer's and my outcome goals, may be vastly different, but the coordination of the team behind us is exactly the same.

In some cases, and I've known it often enough in athletics, it is competition from within the team that will inspire individuals to perform, thus ultimately benefiting the team. Take, for example, the rivalry in almost every rugby team between the forwards and the backs. They are both after the same outcome goal, and they are unavoidably interreliant on each other in attempting actually to achieve that goal. But the rivalry still spurs on each group of players to shine.

The concept of team coordination or, to use a more fashionable term these days, group dynamics, is therefore applicable, not only to the obvious team within a game, like a football or rugby team, but also in the preparation of an individual player. The outcome goal has to be the group task. This is then broken down into various roles, just as the outcome goal has to be achieved by various process goals. Every concept of psychology needs to be applied to the team as a unit, but the following, in particular, need to be analysed in terms of teamwork:

Group composition. The size of the group, and whether there is the correct cohesion and motivation.

Leadership. The relationship between the group members needs to be addressed and the cohesion maintained by the captain or the boss, or whoever is coordinating.

These factors remain the same, whether we are talking about an army regiment entering combat, a secretarial pool in a large corporation, or the 400 metres relay team at the Olympics.

Let's now look at these factors in greater detail.

Group size. In most sports, this number is obviously fixed, but not during the all-important preparatory phases. Whoever said the more the merrier, and two heads are better than one, did not come from the same school of thought as the person who said that while two's company, three's a crowd.

I would tend to agree with the last of these. By subdividing the team during the preparatory phase, the commitment to the group's objectives can be increased. The psychologists Widmeyer, Brawley and Carron investigated this theory in 1990. They organized a series of groups of sports people on a volleyball court, ranging from three people to six, and finally, twelve.

What they found was that, in almost every aspect, the group involving three people benefited most of all. The players' simple enjoyment, together with an effective use of strategies, an increase in responsibility and a sense of better organization were all experienced in the smallest group.

In summing up, it is important in any team, sport or business, to be broken down into smaller groups. Instead of finding yourself pushed to one side in a large group, you should be heavily involved in a much smaller group, which should, initially, work away from the others, before coming back and cohering, bearing in mind that everyone is working towards the same, common goal.

This should banish forever the sight of the miserable boy standing on the touchline at school, with nothing to do. No wonder he doesn't like sport, especially team sports. The moves against team sports in the 1980s, initiated by many local authorities around the country, totally missed the point. Team sport is still about a group of individuals, with individual tasks, who may cohere as a group, but who still have their own roles to play.

Group composition. By this we mean the properties of each individual within the group, and what this group possesses as its factors, which includes professional skills, individual personalities, attitudes and motives, age, sex, and so on.

The theory suggests that everything composite to the team will ultimately have an effect on the team's productivity. Obviously, the better the team's resources, the better it will perform. Oppositional motives can also help here. In other words, how the opposition perceives your team can give you an immediate head start. In previous chapters I have addressed the fact that, in many cases, a perceived performance can manifest itself into an actual performance.

I always remember, as a boy, playing in a rugby team against the local public school. They would always be the better team, and I think that, in part, was because of both teams' attitudes. By the very fact that they were from a public school – which, at the very least, normally considers rugby to be the primary autumn sport, if not the spring term sport too – I assumed that they would naturally be better than us. Therefore, by consulting a skilled coach as part of team preparation, it may not only have the physical benefits of increasing the team's skill, but also increase the perceived ability of your team. Look at Newcastle United, for example. With Kevin Keegan as their team manager, other people's perceptions of the team's ability have been improved. They have made themselves a formidable force, and this can, in part, be explained by the presence of Keegan, whose name and achievements conjure up everything a footballer and a team aspire to.

Group cohesion. Obviously a very important factor in terms of working as a unit. Shared team experiences, a leader's style and communication skills and personality will alter the cohesion within the team. Good communication, training sessions and shared social and sporting experiences will all help to increase the cohesion of a team. If everyone gets along well together then they should perform better as a unit.

This theory may well seem to contradict the point I made earlier about rivalries within a team that can spark individuals to produce better performances. Actually, you can have both aspects within the same team. If people are working directly with each other, like the front row in a rugby scrum, then they have to cohere towards their task, though not necessarily *socially*, in order to be effective. If they don't get along, or are hellbent on outdoing one another, then the end result will be chaos for their small group, and failure for the team as a whole.

At the same time, however, the forwards often form a

collective rivalry against the backs, on and off the field. They both need each other to succeed as a team, but there are times when the forwards or the backs can themselves win the match, when spurred on by their desire to outdo their rivals within the team. There is nothing wrong with inter-rivalry between two or more cohesive groups within a team, as long as each individual or group is edging the other closer to achieving full potential.

Group task. The objective of the group is usually a common and obvious one: i.e. to score a try, a goal or a point. Individual tasks are often less structured than this. Failure to itemize individual tasks can lead to inter-team conflict due to an overlap of duties. But, by giving each individual a very focused task by which he or she can maximize their attention, the overall group task will then be to achieve the desired result.

Each athlete must believe that the way he or she executes a task is far more important than the outcome. Each individual is accountable to the coach, and the coach is the person who will ultimately determine whether each individual has performed the task effectively. Incidentally, the coach is also the person who takes responsibility for failure. It is also very important that each member of the team recognizes the contribution made by the others. As a result, social approval and 'belonging' become additional rewards.

The breakdown of these tasks is a bit like a production line, which has to be the ultimate in team efficiency when working towards an end product. Everyone's role is interrelated. Your role is rendered ineffectual if someone else does not carry out his job properly.

If there are two players on the pitch whose tasks overlap, there will be a lack of productivity because of this waste of resources. Occasionally, two people may have the same role, i.e. to mark a key player on the opposition side, but, even here, the two should form a cohesive group and break down their collective job into individual tasks.

Leadership. All the composite factors to a team – professional skills, personality, motives and attitude – are equally relevant to the team leader.

But, in order to implement tactics and to be able to judge,

assess and direct the group task along the way, the most important factor is communication.

There is far more to a team meshing than a group of individuals just putting on the same shirt. The team that acquires synergy towards each other's individual goals can become the ultimate functioning unit, and should be able to achieve what it aspires to. Sports psychology puts it this way: 'The team's energy should be greater than the sum of that team's individual energy.' In other words, by coming together as a team, each individual's efficiency will improve above and beyond what they are potentially capable of as individuals.

In a sport such as athletics, it is the team meeting prior to the competition itself that is, potentially, the only time that all members come together as a unit. This is therefore the point at which all the potential conflict within the team can be ironed out and the desired environment for the members to communicate can be created. After all, the whole point is one of trying to improve team spirit, and this can only be achieved if the team members trust one another.

SUMMARY ....

If you think of a team being a single unit, then the team should use exactly the same format for preparation as any individual, along the lines outlined in this book, from goal-setting right through to attribution. Preparation must be structured by the leader, and then applied to the individuals within the team.

In the story, the first point about wearing a British team vest for the first time was all about cohesion. It was the cohesion of the team members that gave me the rush of adrenaline, which, in turn, led to increased motivation. Cohesion of the team members means each team member having an interest in how every other member performs. This provides good communication, and a feeling of responsibility.

Confidence naturally followed. Putting on a British vest is a statement in itself, instilling confidence because, although it may be you who throws the javelin, you are made to feel that there is a large team supporting you.

My thinking of Ovett and Coe, who were still competing and winning medals at the time in senior, international athletics, only added to my adrenaline and confidence. These hugely successful sportsmen had also worn the same vest I now found myself wearing. Suddenly, I felt as if we were all on the same side, and even though Coe and Ovett could hardly help my eventual outcome in the competition, it made me feel as if we were now all working as a unit.

It was at the team meeting that I first learnt the importance of breaking a large group down into smaller ones in order to gain greater productivity. I immediately felt as if I had a bigger part to play because my presence was obviously more important in a smaller group. Returning to the team group, the powerful message about competing for our country was all part of the motivation that everybody requires before the day of competition. I then sat down with my particular leader, a member of the team management who had been appointed to look after the throwers. He highlighted what the team required from me.

The overall task was that England wanted to win the international competition. That was then put to one side, just as you do with an outcome goal. The process was to finish first and second, with the other English javelin thrower, ensuring maximum points, which would thus lead to the outcome goal. The party that followed our victory was all part of helping the team to gell together more, to develop an understanding and a trust off the track that could only be positive for our overall team performances in the future.

In the Europa Cup, for example, we see how being part of a team can automatically increase arousal. Pulling on that vest not only instills you with confidence, it also fills you with expectancy. A standard has been set in the past, and it was up to me to continue at the same level. As I said, I did not enjoy this realization at first. It created unwanted tension, which, on other occasions, would have been dealt with by relaxation techniques, focusing on my individual task, and getting down to my own process goals.

In this case, however, I drew an enormous amount of

motivation from seeing Kriss Akabusi unexpectedly win the first event for Britain. I seemed to draw on this extra energy, producing an instant improvement in warm-up. Here was an example of how the team's energy over the Europa Cup-winning weekend was clearly greater than the sum of each individual's energy. This might have been slightly diminished if I had been out there competing just for myself, but the sudden surge of confidence, adrenaline and energy resulted in me winning my particular event, which featured most of the best javelin throwers in the world.

If I am honest, I have never experienced the same feeling in a British team performance since. I am a great believer in the benefits of a good team spirit, and would do anything to improve the sense of family atmosphere that seems to be missing now. But my sport has become more fragmented now, and with the introduction of big money to the highest achievers, everyone is now in it to further themselves.

The problem is that standards have now been set. Silver Medals are no longer good enough. That pressure automatically leads you away from any team feeling. Most athletes, if they are entirely honest with themselves, want not only to be the best in their discipline, but also to achieve the best standard out of all his or her fellow athletes from the same country.

In this competitive environment, the only team that remains is the team that works with the individual athlete towards success. Just like the team of players on a field, you need to enjoy the same trust with your physio and coach, masseur and psychologist. Each has his individual tasks and skills. I do not know, nor am I expected to know every detail of their jobs, but I trust them enough to know that these parts of my preparation, for which they are responsible, are in safe hands. That, to me, is the ultimate in teamwork.

10. CONCLUSION

I said at the beginning of this book that we all possess a mind, and that learning how better to handle it can help achieve much-improved results. Hopefully, you will now understand, judging by my own roller coaster ride through international sport, how true this is.

The mind dominates your every move. Apart from insurmountable physical factors, such as breaking your leg, or just being beaten by a superb performance on the day by an opponent, you will find, just as I did, and have revealed throughout these pages, that your mind is behind every result.

As all the preceding chapters prove, there are many areas of the mind that can cause havoc. This must be addressed, in both the long and the short term. The two golden rules are:

• Never stop addressing all the areas of sports psychology, even when the day of the big event comes round. As my own experiences prove, you can go wrong months before the big event if you fail to address any one psychological aspect. However, you will find that you will need to have the ability not only to work through the ingredients outlined in this book on a long-term basis, but also in the short term, on the day, maybe even during the competition. So, while you need to motivate yourself, set goals, and be able to visualize them way before the event, you have to keep on reminding yourself of all these aspects throughout the process of preparation, right the way up to, and including, the performance.

• Although the book is divided into chapters, which look at the various individual ingredients that make up the sporting psychological process, I am sure you have realized that each topic is interrelated. It is therefore impossible to study the merits of an individual area of sports psychology in isolation from all other aspects. They combine and overlap to make up a vital part of your training for sport or everyday life.

The world, particularly the sporting world, is waking up to the fact that we have never before attempted to maximize the potential of the mind. Sports psychology is a subject that has rapidly increased in appreciation, knowledge and application in a relatively short period of time. For many people, it already forms an integral part of the cutting edge of human endeavour and performance.

Sports psychology is developing all the time. New theories and studies are inevitable as we discover more about the mind. The application of psychology is obviously the key, and however you choose to go about it does not really matter, as long as it improves your performance. Be prepared to try out new methods, armed with the knowledge that they may or may not be the ones for you.

For many others, psychology still sounds very clinical and unattractive, presenting a massively undesirable image, mainly because it is presented as a collection of theories. It is in the transition from theory to practice that psychology has, in the past, often disappointed.

I was young, and had experienced nothing else but success, but another reason why I then went on to suffer from failure was because I had clearly failed to put all the theory I had learned as a sports science student into practice when international sport suddenly produced mental hurdles for me to clear. What chance do others have if even I, who had studied psychology at university, was unable to put the theory into practice until my eyes had been opened, not through studying, but by my own experiences as a competitor? Psychology, as I hope you have now discovered, cannot therefore be ignored.

The idea behind this book is that theory becomes 90 per cent of performing, and every aspect of your performance, from its foundations in training and preparation, to its culmination in the actual performance, is based on good, sound theory.

Although everyday life presents similar problems and challenges to those in sport, most people probably do not sit down and work out how they can rise to meet these challenges by using psychological methods. A growing number of sports people do, however, because they realize that to be a winner in the sporting arena, you have to be, mentally, the strongest competitor.

My own experiences bear obvious testament to this. When you watch a sports event on television, or live in a stadium, the chances are you only see the end result: the goal being scored, the boxer being hit, the Grand Prix driver overtaking, or maybe even the javelin thrower hitting the 90-metre mark. What you don't see, of course, is everything that goes through the competitor's mind during his or her attempt to win the event.

Having read this book, you may now have more of an idea. I have obviously achieved success in world sport but, as every single performer will tell you, such success (and failure) is not secured without an equally stiff battle with your own psyche.

Look at self-doubt, for example. How many people do you know who, in your opinion, are oozing with confidence and belief? In reality, no such person exists. Everyone is as riddled with self-doubt as you and – by the way – me. It is how we choose to deal with this doubt that makes us all different.

For example, Anthony Hopkins, despite the many accolades and films under his belt, admits to suffering an enormous degree of self-doubt. You might think he would be pretty confident at the acting game by now, but of course, it is this anxiety that produces the much better performance.

One of the more common causes of self-doubt comes from worrying about whether you really have worked hard enough beforehand to place yourself in a strong enough position to win – much the same as being worried about whether you have revised sufficiently for an exam.

I fall into this category, even though I work extremely hard at this as a full-time athlete. My concern is exacerbated because the javelin is an extremely physical event, which beats your body up every time you compete. As a result, you tend to rest the week before the actual competition. This has led me to wonder whether I really have put in enough hard work, because my most recent memory is one of doing very little.

In order to counteract this potentially damaging thought process, Dave Collins, the sports psychologist, has come up with an excellent idea that seems to work for me. We have managed to film on video a series of my toughest training sessions during the hard, winter months, making sure that we have a sufficient variation, ranging from running to lifting, throwing to circuit training, and so on. Some of these tend to be extremely gruelling, and have often resulted in me being physically sick.

The idea behind this is that you then watch it on the day of competition. This is the work you have put in to get this far. Even saying it to yourself helps, because it reminds you how much you have stashed away in the bank. As a result, there is a lot there to withdraw on the day of the competition, a realization that immediately eradicates any potential fears, and replaces them with confidence. As a further point, doing this can prevent you from overtraining in those last few weeks or days when your work should already have been completed, which is another common mistake made by even the best sports people; people like Frank Bruno in boxing, and Liz McColgan in athletics, who have both admitted that in the past they have overdone the training, wrongly believing that the more you do, the better you will be, something which has, in the end, affected their performance adversely.

Mind you, such a practice will not completely remove anxiety, and nor should it. They say that if you don't feel any nerves before performing, in whatever capacity, then you will not get close to your potential. This goes back to the chapter on arousal, where we identified the middle-range of arousal as being best for your eventual performance. Too much, or too little, in any walk of life, will create a below-par performance.

Anxiety is an important part of the preparation, in terms of how we increase our concentration. I, for one, am the sort of person who becomes increasingly anxious in the build-up to a competition. The more important the competition, the more anxious I become.

The mind is an extremely complex mechanism, and one we are still far from understanding completely, but I feel the trick with sports psychology is actually to make it simple, using plain techniques, such as the video example already mentioned, to help clear any hurdles. Simply understanding a principle and then applying it can make an immediate 10 per cent difference.

To achieve this using psychology might only take an hour or two, depending on your ability to apply what you have just learnt. But how long would it take you to improve by such a percentage if you just used physical methods to improve? Perhaps a year, maybe even two?

Various sports psychologists I have worked with, and my own experiences, have made me understand how theory can be applied, and appreciate how it can then have an immediate and direct effect on my performance.

The previous chapters, therefore, on motivation, goal-setting, visualization, relaxation and arousal are all designed to outline the basic theory of the science of sports psychology. In the chapters looking at training and warm-up, and competition, the concepts are linked to performance. In the chapter on attribution, the performance is linked back to concept, thereby continuing the psychological cycle.

But how can you now transfer all this theory into practice? Well, it would obviously help if you tried some of the methods provided in this book. What you have to remember though, is that everything in these pages is written from a personal perspective. I do not possess your mind, and you do not possess mine. So it is now your job to try to tap the potential still loitering, undiscovered, in your own mind.

To do this, you need to ask yourself a whole series of questions about yourself. This will initiate the thought process that needs to take place before you can come up with any plan of action necessary to launch your bid to win that competition, achieve that promotion, or whatever else it is that you are aiming for. By asking yourself the following questions, you will begin to understand how you can perform to the best of your potential. This, as already explained, is very Self 1 based. It is therefore not for the day of competition, but for the weeks and months in advance. This will doubly ensure that you are moving in the right direction.

So, what can you actually do to maximize your potential? To do this, we must first try and understand what makes us tick. To whom, for example, would you turn to upon achievement? Is it the same person as when you fail? Try and remember what you consider to be your best ever day in sport or life. What was it that made you perform optimally? Only you know the answers to these questions, and it would be a worthwhile exercise to keep on answering them, and thereby reminding yourself how you best made yourself tick.

If I have the answers to these set questions on a daily basis, then I do not keep on having to ask them of myself. As I have learnt from experience, and through working with sports psychologists, constant questioning can manifest itself as doubt, which, in turn, can lead itself to more questioning, affecting your confidence, your mental strength and, ultimately, your performance.

Once the key questions are dealt with, you must then analyse yourself in greater detail, but always tackling all areas in a positive, constructive way. This prevents any negative feelings and constant self-questioning. Instead, you are saying to yourself: 'Right, how can I improve my performance even more?' Know what you are good and bad at, by testing these individual components, and not by guessing at them. Your perception, after all, may be wrong.

Motivation. Does success scare you as much as failure? Taken as individual experiences, does failure or success scare you? What exactly causes the anxiety in either of these scenarios? What have your previous experiences of success and failure been like – good, or bad? It is wrong automatically to assume that, with everybody, the experience of success is a pleasant one. If you take sports people, many find it difficult, mentally, to repeat success because of the problems, such as expectations, and the pressure they subsequently put on themselves, that the initial experience of success can produce.

If you can get to the bottom of what the actual problem is, and then deal with it, you should then be able to push it to one side. How did you respond to your previous experiences of success and failure?

Consistent movement towards the desired effect can only be fuelled from within, which is why motivation plays an initial and such a crucial role in your road to achieving success.

By organizing your thoughts you can direct them towards the common path more effectively. Organization and preparation are therefore the keys. To do either, we must set goals.

Goal-setting. Do you set goals? If so, are they structured correctly? Do you have an outcome goal that is then broken down into process goals that are attainable on a daily level? In this respect, are they different in the short term and the long term?

What are the most important eight factors that make you good at what you do? Remember the waggon wheel exercise in the chapter on visualization? I certainly subscribe to that particular theory. As you progress, make a point in your training cycle to assess your improvement. Each Friday night, for example, I will sit down with my diary and identify what was good and bad about the previous week's work. Unless you make a point of regularly assessing yourself, and questioning your progress, you will not be able to recognize where you are going right or wrong, and therefore you will be unable to change enough to show a marked progression.

How do you react if you fail to reach your goal, even your daily goal? Remember, if your goals are structured correctly, then reaching a process goal on a daily basis should automatically mean that you also reach your eventual outcome goal. How do you reward yourself when you have achieved your goals? What do you do if you achieve your outcome goal before you were expecting to? This is something I had to deal with at a young age. I progressed very quickly to the top in my sport on a worldwide basis. Once I had reached the stage I was aiming for, it became increasingly difficult to find the necessary amount of motivation to carry on at the same level.

With proper and structured goal-setting, I now have an outcome goal, which is to win a global Gold Medal. Winning the Silver Medal in the 1995 World Championships was a step towards this, and now I hope to reach my outcome goal by becoming the Olympic champion. The point is, that if you achieve your initial outcome goals, there will always be new outcome goals to set in life.

Of course, you do not have to answer all these questions, but you do need to have a clear picture in your mind of what your various goals should be, and how you must reach them. If you are to be structured about this, and feel confident enough about your progress, then you can move on to examining your performance through visualization.

Visualization. The term used for seeing yourself perform in your mind. Can you do this? If not, do not underestimate the power and effect of this mental imagery. If you can visualize, what can you see? Is it at normal speed, and are there any gaps in the process? Are you easily distracted? If so, then you should practice more, possibly on a daily basis. I believe that I can visualize well, but I still have three, good sessions a week to make it even better.

Do you always see a successful outcome? Is it always a positive picture you see? The theory suggests that it is beneficial to do exactly this. Give yourself positive not negative commands. In other words, instead of saying I must not, tell yourself instead that you must or you will, directing your attention to a positive state of mind.

Try using the same word each time you visualize in order to create a response. Use these key words to create control over your anxiety and concentration. The key word initiates your response. If you have a small library of key words, you should be able to initiate your response to whatever barrier suddenly appears in your way. A key word can open up a whole chapter of feelings and rhythms.

In my case, the words 'relaxed arms' play an important part. If I feel anxious and stressed, which in turn makes me lose my concentration and control, the key words 'relaxed arms' come into good use. I relax my arms when I begin my relaxation techniques, and by saying this to myself, it automatically initiates the whole relaxation procedure. The physical response to this is that I lose tension in my neck and shoulders, and everything seems to slow down. This is exactly what I want.

Are there any changes in your visualization when you actually compete? If so, what are they? If these are not seen as positive changes, then they may well need working on. It is at the competition that you want to perform to your optimum level, so when we visualize this, we must create a series of positive images.

Training and warm-up. Training and warm-up is the process of attuning your mind so that it can act in synchronization with your body, which will maximize your performance. During training and warm-up, do you visualize? Do you think about posture and rhythm? Have you thought about preparing your emotions for the big day of competition? If not, maybe you should try this by using visualization, which, hopefully, will identify in advance what is likely to make you most anxious.

The theory suggests that constantly visualizing something makes us less anxious. If you improve, then you are closer to being ready to perform. If you are not improving, then you need to find out why. Again, referring back to the waggon wheel technique, grade yourself, and try to work out how you can get your score closer to 10. Are these differences the basis of your training?

What is the difference between your training and competition, both physically and mentally? Are these changes positive? What effect do other people around you have on your training? Are there any places you do not like training? If so, why? Visualizing a particular scenario that you don't like and which therefore makes you anxious should help to reduce such stress by introducing positive cues to increase confidence.

Arousal. Remember, everybody is scared and anxious when they come to compete. Just because someone may appear to be better than you, at least on paper, does not mean that they are necessarily more confident. Is anxiety a controllable factor for you when it comes to competing? When do you become more anxious?

Just to underline this very important point, you must not only be positive about your own lack of confidence, but you must also recognize that your opponents are wracked with exactly the same doubts as you. Gain strength from this fact. This is the same whether in a sports competition or vying for a job.

I have expressed doubt in my ability on a number of occasions, despite all the success I have achieved in international sport. I know that this is the case with all my opposition, and this increases my motivation, my confidence and my concentration.

Have you ever choked? If, like me, the answer is yes, analyse the reasons behind it. It is hard to admit this failure to yourself, and much easier to find external factors. The latter case would be a mistake, because if you fail to recognize why you made mistakes, you are unlikely to progress.

For me, that day was when I wanted it most of all, in Tokyo in 1991. My desire could not be questioned, but the occasion affected my arousal, making me anxious to the point where it impaired my performance. This is a typical response when referring to the optimal arousal theory.

What would you say was the level of your arousal on your best day when, presumably, everything went to plan? Can you mimic this when you visualize? If so, do so when you visualize. Arousal can often conjure up a make-or-break situation, because the most likely time to experience either overarousal or under-arousal is on the day of competition. As I have found in the past, there is a very fine line between performing at the height of our excitement, holding our concentration and therefore producing our peak, and totally messing up, either through letting excited emotions take control, or through not being able to lift ourselves up to the required height necessary to perform closer to optimum level. If we have covered all these questions, and therefore know the answers to all possible scenarios before the event, then it is very possible that no surprises will suddenly be thrown up on the big day. As I have repeatedly said throughout this book, it is all part of good preparation.

What is it about a future task that makes you anxious? Is it less stressful if you break the task down into a sequence of shorter, simpler tasks within the main one. Visualize them individually, and then place the pieces together to form the complete task.

Are you ever underaroused? If I am, I find the best method of pulling myself together is to ask myself if failure is going to bother me. What effect will it have on my pride, my ambitions, my lifestyle? How will I face my family and friends if I fail? Do I care about this? By asking yourself such questions you may well find yourself in a position of having increased your motivation and enthusiasm.

Relaxation. How good is your ability to relax and concentrate? Remember, they both control your ability to perform to your optimum level. Anxiety often turns itself into tension, especially in the shoulders, neck and jaw. This is a clear example of how a negative mental state can surface as a physical problem. It is your ability to counteract this that could mean the difference between winning and losing.

Can you block out unwanted distractions? What makes you concentrate most? If you know the answer to this question, then use the method you have just identified whenever you compete. Is your training or job interesting? What could make it more interesting? Is making those changes possible? If they will not distract from your process goals, then think about introducing these changes. The theory, after all, states that an increase in interest is directly related to an increase in concentration.

Can you perform the relaxation technique outlined in the chapter on competition? If not, then put it into your weekly training schedule, paying particular attention first to centering, before moving on to the actual relaxation techniques. I know from personal experience that this is an extremely useful tool for decreasing arousal.

Competition. What was the difference between the two days when you got it absolutely right and completely wrong? Note as many differences as you can. Draw a line down the middle of a piece of paper, denoting your best and worst days. What were your physical and mental differences on both days? How exactly did you prepare for both days? What you will eventually see written down on both halves of the piece of paper should tell its own story.

How often do you get it right? What percentage of the time do you achieve this? Do you often walk away from your task with a feeling of underachievement? If so, why? Perhaps the goals you have set yourself are too high. Are you self-critical when you are performing? If so, take another look at the Self 1/Self 2 theory, as expressed by Timothy Gallwey, in the chapter on attribution.

Do you know the music to your event? If not, try to learn it. Do you enjoy competing? If you don't, ask yourself why and then try to ascertain whether those problems can be eradicated. What could you do to improve your mind on the day of competition? Once you have finished competing, the theory of attribution needs to be understood so that you can learn effectively from your experiences.

Attribution. The theories of attribution are based around understanding whether you can attribute your performance to you or to something else. Who do you blame when you fail? Is it the same person as when you succeed? Is it you and you alone? If this is the case, then the theory suggests that you are being very honest with yourself and thus stand a better chance of improving. Remember another key point to this book – you can't change the past, but you can change the way you react to it.

Being completely honest with yourself will immediately prevent you from wasting any more time, or opportunities than necessary. In the short term, in sports such as tennis or golf, this will mean the prevention of the loss of more points or strokes for the same reason as your original failure. If you fail to attribute correctly why you hook your tee shot, you will continue to do so until you address the problem correctly and honestly.

Teamwork. If you are part of a team, are you aware of your individual task? Do you know your overall team's task? Do you feel part of a stronger force by being in a team? If so, then this is optimal for team spirit and performance.

If you are a coach or a manager, have you considered factors such as group composition, and whether conflicts and/or cohesion will lead to a better team performance? Does everyone in your team know his or her individual task? I remember being a part of basketball and soccer teams when I was a youngster. I was not particularly proficient at either, and this is because I did not know my own task well enough. I was unaware of how my task interrelated with the tasks of my team-mates, and did not know what we should have expected of each other.

If people are aware of this, they can channel their energy far more effectively. I am sure I could have applied myself more effectively if my task had been spelled out to me. I fear that there is a great waste of sporting talent in this country at school, at least in team sports, because individual tasks have not been made clear.

All the above is therefore crucial to a better understanding of the mind. It seems an awful lot, but each area flows into every other area, reminding you each time of the various requirements of psychology. If you can crack at least some of this, then you will be giving yourself a better chance of succeeding at whatever event you choose.

This is what I intend to do for the Olympics. I realize that, by the very nature of my position in world javelin throwing, and my previous achievements in major championships, I stand a chance (as do a small number of my rivals), of winning the Olympic Gold Medal in Atlanta. What I must do, between now and the qualifying event for the final, is to give myself the best shot. To do this, to be as mentally prepared as possible, I must draw on all my experiences from the past and then direct them towards the future. Sports psychology offers me a language to be able to formulate this in an extremely comprehensive manner.

As I have said before, self-doubt, despite my success, has always been one of my more prominent problems. After talking this through with Dave Collins, the sports psychologist I work with at present, we concluded that my self-doubt is derived from the fear of losing. If this is the case, then what can I do to combat this – which I will need to do if I want to give myself a serious chance of that Olympic Gold Medal?

Our answer has been to make a list of everything – and I mean everything – that could go wrong between now and the very last throw of the Olympic final. I wasn't sure about this to begin with. All my preparation has always been positive and suddenly I was asking myself to look at negative aspects. It didn't strike me as a natural way forward. But now it makes a great deal of sense.

The trick is to make such a list a long way off from the actual event so that it won't be fresh in your mind on the day of competition. This also gives you enough time to tick off every entry on the list in the build-up to the Games in good time.

I have to be very honest with myself when making this list, marking down even the most trivial items that might be contenders for throwing my mind off my task. At the 1988 World Junior Championships in Sudbury, my mind talked me out of a Gold Medal after a series of ridiculously irrelevant events threw me off my task? The very fact that things have gone wrong in the past means that this could happen again, so make reference to *everything* that has gone wrong in the past. I will therefore be writing down possibilities such as: Jan Zelezny produces a 90-metre throw in the first round of the Olympic final; I'm in ninth place with just one throw left to lift myself up at least a place and qualify for the second half of the final; I have left a part of my kit behind in the hotel; there is a torrential downpour of rain; there is a heat wave; even a crisis in my family. It doesn't matter if your list is pages long, as long as you can deal with every aspect in time.

Another area I intend to improve on in time for the Olympics is my visualization, and my ability to 'hear the music'. I know from previous experiences that when I can hear the music well,

I usually compete well. Three times a week, I will be visualizing what I consider to be not my longest, but my best ever throw – with which I first broke the world record in Stockholm. I will be reintroducing as vivid a picture of that night in my mind as possible, including the sights, sounds and smells of the throw.

I have also learnt how to visualize at the correct pace, thanks mainly to Calvin Morris and his colleagues at Crewe and Alsager College. They have managed to digitize my foot contact with the ground during that Stockholm throw. The rhythm of my foot contact with the ground is given a beat. I now have a tape of my run-up during that throw. This is the music I need to re-enact such a performance. Each time my foot hits the ground the tape beeps, repeating itself faster and faster as my run along the run-up area increases in speed, before I launch the javelin. I now know this series of beeps like I know my favourite pop record.

It may sound difficult, but it is actually extremely easy, because it is precisely the same principle as listening to a familiar song on the radio. If the tune was a slightly different version, you would immediately notice, even if it boiled down to a different drum roll or guitar solo. In other words, when you listen to one of your favourite songs, you know it so well that you don't just know the words, but every, individual note.

It is the same with my digitized foot-contact tape. When visualizing the perfect run-up, I can immediately incorporate the memory of this tape into my mind. If I were slightly to mistime a step in my run-up during visualization, I would immediately notice, just as you would notice a different note in a song.

Another exercise I believe well worth doing as part of my preparation for the Olympics is to twice pretend to be competing in the Olympic final. This will be undertaken a good few months in advance of the real event, in order to give me time to make any necessary changes that are needed. I will go through the whole process of the day, from waking up, to eating, to warming up, and then, finally, to competing. The point of this is, hopefully, obvious. By the time I reach the Olympic final, I will have already been through it twice already this year, living through every aspect of such a day. Of course, I have already been through the day of an Olympic final for real, but that was four years ago, and I believe it is well worth my while reminding myself of such an experience before I have to go through it again. It will therefore be a couple of dress rehearsals for me, in order to overcome what could be one of the massive hurdles on the day.

Writing this book has also played a part in my preparation for the Olympics. It has forced me to transcribe my thoughts, putting them into an order that will prove invaluable to me. I've gone through each year of my career, accounting for success and failure in equal measure and, I'd like to think, in honest measures. This has given me a much clearer picture of what is necessary in my preparations for the Olympics. For the first time, I have been able fully to assess my whole career, and have been able to identify how I have managed to succeed, and how I can continue to learn from my mistakes.

Learning from your own mistakes is an invaluable exercise, but it is by far preferable if you can learn from other people's mistakes. It is less energetic, and certainly less painful, so by reading this book, and seeing where I have gone wrong, you may not fall into the same self-made potholes that I have.

If, however, you think that this book has *all* the answers, then I am afraid to tell you that you are mistaken. For a start, nothing is guaranteed, especially when it comes to sport. All you can do is to make it as likely as possible that you will succeed.

The other point to reiterate, in a final conclusion, is that this book provides a host of instances from personal experience. The theories may well be accepted, but the practice, as outlined in these pages, has been very much geared towards Steve Backley. The various mental decisions I have taken to rectify my problems have been right for me, but that by no means necessarily makes them right for you. It may well be that after trying some of my methods, you decide that they are not for you.

That's absolutely okay. This is not a textbook guide. This is purely designed to outline what you should be doing to discover how your very own, individual character can get it right for the big day. There is only one of you in this world, and it is ultimately up to you to discover the best ways of becoming mentally strong using, hopefully, some of my methods.

I must remind you again of the untapped potential we all possess – yes, that means you too. I do not believe that I have ever been massively gifted when it comes to physical ability in sport, despite my size. I firmly believe that I could walk down the street today and see someone with at least as much physical ability as me. But I have, on occasions, been able to tap into what ability I possess, drawing a little closer to my potential possibly than others have done, which has resulted in success. Nobody can get it right all the time, but with simple application, we can all improve our performances by getting better acquainted with the mind.

So, all that remains for me to do is to wish you the very best of luck with your own mental preparations. If you can get these right, you have a much better chance of successfully reaching your goals. And that is what sports psychology is all about.

APPENDIX

···

STEVE BACKLEY'S RECORD:

1987: European Junior Championships: Gold Medal.
1988: World Junior Championships: Silver Medal.
1989: Europa Cup: Gold Medal.
World Cup: Gold Medal.
World Student Games: Gold Medal.
Grand Prix: 1st in Javelin
1990: Commonwealth Games: Gold Medal.
European Championships: Gold Medal.
World Record: Stockholm, 89.58 metres.
World Record: Crystal Palace, 90.98 metres.
IAAF Athlete of the Year.
1991: World Student Games: Gold Medal.
World Championships: 15th
British and Commonwealth Record: Sheffield, 91.36 metres.
1992: Olympic Games: Bronze Medal.
World Record: Auckland, 91.46 metres.
1993: World Championships: 4th
1994: European Championships: Gold Medal.
Commonwealth Games: Gold Medal.
World Cup: Gold Medal.
1995: World Championships: Silver Medal.

INDEX